The Library Services and

Construction Act:
An Historical Overview From
The Viewpoint of Major Participants

FOUNDATIONS IN LIBRARY AND
INFORMATION SCIENCE, VOLUME 18

Editor: Robert D. Stueart, *Dean, Graduate School of Library and*
         Information Science, Simmons College

Foundations in
LIBRARY AND INFORMATION SCIENCE

A Series of Monographs, Texts and Treatises

Series Editor: **Robert D. Stueart**
Dean Graduate School of Library and Information Science
Simmons College, Boston

When you look back over the 25 years and you see what has been accomplished throughout the country, it is really a great thrill to see how libraries have progressed. . . .We have come a long way. . . .I hate to think that we are close to the point of. . .going backward. . . .I believe in the larger systems. . . .I believe in the metropolitan libraries. . . .And we have got to have the funding from the federal government. It is the federal government's responsibility, and the states' and the localities', to fund the libraries so that we will have a vital library service in this country that will be available to every single individual.

Julia Bennett Armistead
Former Director
ALA Washington Office
Taped interview, May 4, 1982

The Library Services and Construction Act:

An Historical Overview From The Viewpoint of Major Participants

by   EDWARD G. HOLLEY
Dean, School of Library Science
University of North Carolina
at Chapel Hill Library

ROBERT F. SCHREMSER
School of Library Science
University of North Carolina
at Chapel Hill Library

 **JAI PRESS INC.**

Greenwich, Connecticut   *London, England*

Library of Congress Cataloging in Publication Data

Holley, Edward G.
  The Library Service and Construction Act.

  (Foundations in library and information science ; v. 18)
  Bibliography: p.
  Includes index.
  1. Library legislation—United States. I. Schremser
Robert F. II. Title. III. Series.
  KF4315.H64   1983   344.73′092   83-48088
  ISBN 0-89232-410-4   347.30492

KF4315
H64
1983

Copyright © 1983 JAI PRESS INC.
36 Sherwood Place
Greenwich, Connecticut 06830

JAI PRESS INC.
3 Henrietta Place
London WC2E 8LU
England

ISBN Number 0-89232-410-4
Library of Congress Catalog Card Number 83-048088
Manufactured in the United States of America

CONTENTS

List of Tables

Acknowledgments

The authors owe a debt to many persons for their assistance in the development of this book. For the impetus we give credit to Bessie Moore, without whose prodding the LSCA Oral History Project would never have been undertaken. Ms. Moore, Eileen Cooke, John Lorenz, and Roger McDonough read the manuscript and made a number of helpful suggestions.

Robert Klassen, Ray Fry, and Dorothy Kittel at the U.S. Department of Education have maintained their interest in our project far beyond the call of their official duties. We thank Ms. Kittel, particularly, for her careful reading of the manuscript and for her encouragement.

My secretary, Marie Hyde, will be happy to see this project appear between hard covers. The typing of corrections, emendations, and rewriting must certainly have taxed her patience, though she has always responded promptly and cheerfully to one more review of the contents. Let me also thank Frances McCoy, Administrative Assistant, for her participation at one crucial point. As the project went to press, my research assistant, Kathleen Brown, was especially helpful in checking both the text and the bibliography—the latter a trying experience for all. Ruth Gambee prepared a fine index in record time for which I am grateful. Also thanks to Sally Whelan, JAI Production Department, whose meticulous attention to editing the manuscript saved us from many mistakes and whose designing of the book met fully our expectations.

To the participants we owe most of all. This is their story. Our thanks to all thirteen witnesses to the LSCA record: Elizabeth Hughey Arline, Julia Bennett Armistead, Eileen Cooke, Carl Elliott, Emerson Greenaway, Paul Howard, Mary Allen Jolley, Germaine Krettek, Charles W.

Lee, John Lorenz, Roger McDonough, Bessie Moore, and Evelyn Day
Mullen. Their interest and enthusiasm have spurred us on.

Finally to JAI Press for their willingness to make the revised edition
of our report to the U.S. Department of Education available to the library
community.

Edward G. Holley

Photographs

1. Alexandria, Va., Participants in the Video Taping Sessions
(left to right: Roger McDonough, John Lorenz, Eileen Cooke,
Paul Howard, Elizabeth Hughey Arline, Charles Lee)

2. Chapel Hill Participants in the Video Taping Sessions
(left to right: Emerson Greenaway, Evelyn Mullen, Bessie Moore,
Ed Holley, Germaine Krettek, Carl Elliot)

3. Co-Author Robert Schremser with Congressman Carl Elliot

4. Elizabeth Hughey Arline and John Lorenz—
They Administered LSCA Programs

5. Roger McDonough, New Jersey State Librarian and Consultant for LSCA Projects

6. Paul Howard: First Director of the ALA Washington Office

7. Charles W. Lee: Assistant to Senator Wayne Morse and
Various Senate Committees and Lobbyist for Educational Programs

8. Evelyn Day Mullen: Alabama State Librarian and USOE Program
Director

9. Moderator Edward G. Holley

10. Bessie B. Moore: Initiator of the LSCA Oral History Project

11. Emerson Greenaway: Father of the Construction Clause of LSCA

12. Germaine Krettek: One of ALA's and Washington's
Most Effective Lobbyists

13. Congressman Carl Elliott:
He Led the Fight to Suspend the Rules in 1960

14. Julia Bennett in a Characteristic Pose

15. Bessie Moore Presents Julia Bennett a Wrist Watch,
Miami Beach Conference, 1956

16. The White House after Signing of the LSCA Bill in 1964
(left to right: Bessie Moore, Emerson Greenaway,
President Lyndon Johnson, and Cora Paul Bomar)

17. Congressman Carl Elliot and Evelyn Day Mullen:
A Bookmobile Stop in Alabama, 1955

18. Eileen Cooke, Director of the ALA Washington Office,
with Longtime LSCA Supporter, Senator Jacob Javits of New York

19. Paul Howard, Charles Lee and Robert Schremer

20. Legislative Day, April 3, 1979, National Library Week
(left to right: Eileen D. Cooke, Frances Pletz,
Rep. William D. Ford, Margaret Thomas and Francis X. Scannell)

Chapter 1

Introduction

In 1981 the Library Services and Construction Act (LSCA) celebrated its twenty-fifth anniversary. To recognize the occasion, the American Library Association (ALA) asked Fred Glazer, West Virginia State Librarian, to prepare a multimedia presentation for its annual conference in San Francisco. With his accustomed flair, Glazer created an extravaganza highlighting the events of the last twenty-five years and the impact of LSCA on libraries and their users.

That late afternoon program on June 29, 1981 was a time of enjoyment, exhiliration, and appreciation for LSCA's achievements. Just prior to Glazer's presentation, Carma Zimmerman Leigh, former State Librarian of California, read a paper entitled "The Beginnings of Federal Library Legislation with Specific Reference to the Library Services and Construction Act." Leigh noted the importance of the issues, problems, and solutions still remaining after twenty-five years, but also urged pride in LSCA's accomplishments. She ended her remarks with a call to arms: "You are always on the side of the public interest. Be hopeful, and, above all, *persist, be stubborn,* and *be tough*" (*ALA Yearbook,* 1982, p. 285).

This celebration of LSCA's twenty-five years led a number of individuals to renewed appreciation for the significance of this pioneering educational legislation. One person, especially, was stirred to action by the program. Bessie Moore, Vice Chairperson of the National Commission on Libraries and Information Science, stopped Ed Holley in the hall and urged him to undertake an oral history project to record the memories of the major participants in the battle for federal aid to libraries. She said, "You ought to get us old dogs together and record our impressions before we pass from the scene. . . . And you're just the one to do it!" In his best dean's manner Ed told her he thought she had a wonderful idea

1

and wouldn't it be great if someone could be found to fund such a project? As so often happens to deans, he then dismissed the idea from his mind, despite a similar enthusiastic recommendation from Eileen Cooke, Director of ALA's Washington office. Deans and historians, after all, generally have more projects than they can say grace over.

Upon his return to Chapel Hill, Holley received an inquiry from the U.S. Department of Education. Would he be willing to undertake a modest LSCA oral history project under the auspices of the department's small grants program? He immediately knew what had happened. Moore and Cooke had taken their idea to Education Department officials and convinced them of the value of such a project. They already knew that a UNC doctoral student, Robert Schremser, was planning a dissertation on former Congressman Carl Elliott and his role in library legislation. Wasn't the University of North Carolina at Chapel Hill an appropriate place for LSCA's oral history to be recorded and preserved? It was and is. Moral of this story: Never underestimate Bessie Moore.

From the very beginning we intended the scope of this oral history project to be limited. Even if one had a massive grant there would be little likelihood of completing a definitive history in the amount of time available. Thus we wanted to bring together, or interview separately, ten to twelve persons who had a major influence on federal library legislation. We expected these individuals to provide us with new insight into the persons and events connected with the LSCA and its predecessor, the Library Services Act (LSA).

Our basic plan was simple: We would bring together five or six major participants in Chapel Hill, N.C., and in the Washington, D.C. area for two or three days and, as far as possible, interview them individually and collectively. We would prepare ourselves, as interviewers, with basic information on the chronology of the act from various articles and books which had been written about the legislation. We would prepare an extensive bibliography and final report of the project for distribution to interested persons. We would collect from the participants and others a comprehensive body of information which other researchers could use, for example, photos, scrapbooks, and other tapes.

Although not a part of the original plan, the results of our videotaping were so successful that we will also make available to colleagues copies of the videotapes of the group sessions produced for us by the UNC Instructional Development, Media and Instructional Support Center and the Department of Educational Media Services of the Alexandria, Virginia, Public School System. Our special thanks go to the production staffs of these two studios, especially to Richard I. Palmer at Chapel Hill and Dale Brown, Director of Educational Media Services, Alexandria, Virginia, Public School System.

Whom have we included in this oral history project? From the very beginning we were interested in interviewing the major figures but realized that it would not be possible to reach all of them. We were certain that we wanted to include a variety of persons from different backgrounds and geographic areas. Directors of the ALA Washington office were an obvious choice. We were fortunate to be able to include Paul Howard, who was the first director, from 1945-49; Germaine Krettek, 1957-72; and Eileen Cooke, 1972-date. Julia Bennett Armistead (1951-57) was unable to attend the taping sessions but Schremser interviewed her twice at her home in Knoxville, Tennessee. Other persons who were included in our two major taping sessions are noted below.

In Chapel Hill on January 8-9, 1982, we interviewed on videotape former Congressman Carl Elliott, who had chaired the House subcommittee to extend the act in 1960 and had been a strong supporter of library legislation during his sixteen years in the House (1948-64); Emerson Greenaway, a former Director of the Free Library of Philadelphia, ALA Legislation Committee Chair, and ALA President, 1958-59; Germaine Krettek; Bessie Moore, lay leader and for many years Chairwoman of the Arkansas Library Commission; and Evelyn Day Mullen, former Alabama State Librarian and staff member of the U.S. Office of Education (USOE). We also interviewed on audiotape Congressman Elliott's former assistant, Mary Allen Jolley, who was also the staff assistant for the National Advisory Commission on Libraries from 1966-68. The two-hour panel on videotape provided us with an important historical record, especially of some of the behind-the-scenes political maneuvering in which the participants were involved.

In Alexandria, Virginia, on February 12, 1982, we interviewed six individuals: Paul Howard; Eileen Cooke; Roger McDonough, former New Jersey State Librarian and former Chair, ALA Legislation Committee, and ALA President, 1968-69; Charles W. Lee, former staff member to various Senate committees and staff member of the Committee for Full Funding of Education Programs; John Lorenz, former Deputy Librarian of Congress and former Director, Library Services Branch, USOE; and Elizabeth Hughey Arline, former North Carolina State Librarian and former USOE staff member.

Holley was the moderator for the videotaping sessions. There are two Chapel Hill tapes of one hour each and three Alexandria tapes constituting two hours and twenty minutes. By any objective measure these videotapes constitute the principal outcome of the project and are a valuable source of information for future studies of LSCA and federal library legislation. Because of the background, experience, and long involvement of these individuals with library legislation in general, and with LSCA and LSA particularly, they were able to provide not only important insights into the failures and successes of the act but also an evaluation of its impact upon American citizens. Listening to the responses of the participants and their interaction with each other, Holley was struck by the similarity between the questions posed initially by opponents to the act and those raised by opponents of continuing this legislation today. The chief question, of course, is "Does the federal government have a role to play in the support of library programs?"

What follows in this report is an historical overview of LSCA from the perspective of those who were involved in the program from its beginning to the present time. While the story cannot be regarded as a definitive history, it is a contribution *toward* a history which can be written with the help of the records we have collected. Moreover, we have attempted to be accurate in our presentation of the facts and our report surely does provide a framework for subsequent histories. As much as possible, we have tried to capture the flavor of the times, the political maneuvering, the sidestepping of controversial subjects, and the interplay of personalities during the past three decades. Obviously the written word does this less well than do the videotapes. We certainly recommend that interested persons view the tapes themselves to hear what it was like to call a southern legislator out of a committee meeting, or beard a chairman in his office, or hear the rural mail carrier in Pikeville, Kentucky testify before the National Advisory Commission. One comes away from these tapes with an enhanced appreciation for the dedication and sense of excitement that librarians and their friends so consistently demonstrated over three decades.

One more caveat. The focus of this effort has been on the development of the legislation, its first renewal in 1960, and its expansion during the Great Society years. Much of the story of the seventies remains to be told, though we have not hesitated to comment on some facets of the Nixon, Ford, Carter, and Reagan years. Nor did our panelists hesitate to speak their minds about the future of LSCA and other federal library legislation. For the light their comments shed upon such matters, we can be grateful to these pioneers. As the "old timers" pass from the scene, their story needs to be recorded for further investigation. We hope policy studies, legislative histories, and biographical efforts will benefit from their reminiscences.

The authors express their appreciation to all who assisted in this project. They have done so unselfishly, enthusiastically, and without compensation. The results should enhance our own sense of perspective and encourage others to continue the process begun here.

Chapter 2

Early Attempts at Federal Legislation for Libraries

The story of the American Library Association's efforts to secure federal legislation for libraries began in the twenties and thirties. Those efforts were often attended by major battles within the Association itself. Librarians shared the widespread societal distrust of a federal role in supporting education, of which libraries were seen as an important element. Most citizens, including many librarians, regarded the support of education as a local and state responsibility. Therefore, even though the ALA Council approved a resolution in support of federal aid as early as 1921, the emergence of an ALA legislative program in the mid-thirties met with strong opposition.

The Denver conference in 1935 may have been the high watermark of librarians' opposition to federal aid. The state library associations of Connecticut, Massachusetts, and New Jersey all presented resolutions against federal aid to libraries. Resolutions of approval were received from the Indiana, New York, and Wisconsin library associations. Strong support also came from such leaders as Carleton B. Joeckel, who wrote one of the major national plans (1938); ALA Executive Secretary Carl Milam; University of Chicago Dean Louis Round Wilson; and Mary Utopia Rothrock, Director of the Tennessee Valley Authority's library system. The proponents early focused their efforts on establishing a library service unit in the U.S. Office of Education.

The Library Services Division became a reality in 1938 and provided the stimulus for much of the subsequent expansion of library activities. Many observers of the Washington scene have noted that the library world was fortunate in the Division's first director, Ralph Dunbar, who

5

came to Washington from his post of Associate Librarian at Iowa State College and remained the head of the Library Services Division for the next twenty years. The Library Services Division became the focal point for the gathering of statistics, the production of studies and surveys, and the promotion of library development. Dunbar apparently had an encyclopedic grasp of the status of U.S. libraries. He was often effective behind the scenes in providing information needed both by librarians and their legislative allies. Eventually this office became the Library Services Branch of USOE and assumed administrative responsibility for the Library Services Act and its successor, the Library Services and Construction Act.

Bills for federal aid to education surfaced regularly in the next two decades. Libraries were first included in an omnibus education bill in 1938. As early as 1939, in a pamphlet titled *Federal Aid for Libraries*, the American Library Association tried to defuse opposition by coming out strongly for *state control* of the hoped-for federal funds. The principle of state and local control was firmly embedded in subsequent legislation, though time has tended to erode the concept in implementation. Changing national priorities in the late sixties and early seventies led to a stronger sense of national direction. One should note, however, that the early efforts to secure federal funds for library development were always coupled with a strong commitment to assure state and local plans for their implementation.

World War II interrupted the focus on federal legislation for libraries, but ALA continued its national planning efforts during the years 1940-45. By the time World War II ended, the Association was prepared to launch a major effort to obtain federal funds for the development of rural public libraries.

THE ALA WASHINGTON OFFICE

Relocation of the American Library Association's headquarters to Washington, D.C. has been promoted by many in the library world for years, but opposition to that sentiment has prevailed, and ALA headquarters remains in Chicago. Yet by 1945, the increasing relationships of the Association with federal and foundation officials had made an on-the-scenes person in Washington essential. Doubtless the establishment of an International Relations Office in D.C. during the war years had reinforced the desirability of having an ALA representative there. Many librarians made the trek to the nation's capital in behalf of a variety of interests. Included among that number were ALA officials Carl Milam,

Charles Harvey Brown, Keyes Metcalf, and Paul Howard, the Chair of the ALA Federal Relations Committee.

Chronically short of funds to support its multitudinous activities, the ALA decided to raise money from its membership for temporary support of a Washington Office. The original suggestion had been made by Althea Warren, Director of the Los Angeles County Public Library and ALA President, 1943-44. The ALA Council approved a Library Development Fund drive late in 1944. By the end of 1945 ALA had accumulated gifts of $87,645 toward an original goal of $105,000. The success of the drive encouraged ALA officers. The Fund supported a modest ALA Washington Office until the fall, 1949.

As described by Paul Howard, the first director, the Washington Office began as a one-person operation. Howard used a Washington stenographer in his hotel to type the draft of the first piece of library legislation which was to become the Public Library Service Demonstration Bill. Soon secretarial staff was needed. A legislative network was inaugurated (consisting of state librarians and others interested in library extension), and formal lobbying began.

Initially, the Washington Office kept in touch with the profession at large through a column, "Federal Relations News," in the monthly *ALA Bulletin*. In January, 1949, that column was succeeded by the *ALA Washington Newsletter*, which kept interested persons informed on federal legislation of concern to the library community. A complete file of the *ALA Washington Newsletter* provides an indispensable source for any history of federal library legislation.

The Washington Office was concerned not only with development of new federal legislation but also with other matters such as the disposal of surplus property, postal legislation, and the acquisition of government documents by American libraries. However, the Public Library Services Demonstration Bill became the major focus of Paul Howard's activities.

THE BATTLE FOR THE PUBLIC LIBRARY SERVICE DEMONSTRATION BILL (1949-50)

Librarians across the country had been impressed by the library demonstration projects initiated by Essae Martha Culver, State Librarian of Louisiana, in the twenties. This program, funded initially by the Carnegie Corporation, included provisions for state and local funding after the parish demonstration libraries had proved their value to the citizens. As subsequent writers have noted, this Louisiana project became a precursor of the library demonstration bill.

Developments in the thirties, especially surveys and studies, also supported arguments for federal legislation. The theme of these arguments can be stated simply: once library service was demonstrated, citizens would become receptive to making that service a permanent part of local funding. Demonstrations in a variety of forms became a part of the southern scene where the Rosenwald Fund and the Tennessee Valley Authority provided strong support. Bessie Moore, Carl Elliott, and Roger McDonough also mentioned the stimulus to library programs provided by the New Deal's Works Projects Administration. Added to these efforts were the pioneering books of Tommie Dora Barker, *Libraries of the South* (1936); Gretchen Schenk, *County and Regional Libraries* (1954), which encouraged rural library development; and Louis Round Wilson, *Geography of Reading* (1938), as well as Joeckel's *Library Services* (1938), which was prepared for the President's Advisory Committee on Education.

Still, in promoting the Public Library Service Demonstration Bill, Paul Howard faced a formidable obstacle from opponents who viewed federal aid to libraries, like federal aid to education, as unconstitutional. He was conscious of the need to work with prospective opponents as well as proponents of the legislation. He worked closely with George Smith, an administrative assistant to the Republican Policy Committee in the U.S. Senate, to allay fears about unconstitutionality. Basically his aim was the development of a bill that would meet the objections of Senator Robert A. Taft of Ohio, Mr. Republican himself. Taft opposed federal aid to education and to libraries on the basis that they were constitutionally a state and local responsibility. Although Howard never succeeded in obtaining Taft's support, he did succeed in reducing the level of the Senator's opposition. At one point, when the bill came up for unanimous consent on the Senate calendar, Taft reportedly turned to Senator George Aiken, one of the bill's sponsors, and said, "I think I'll take a walk."

Sponsorship of the original bill came from Congresswoman Emily Taft Douglas of Illinois in the House and Senator Lister Hill of Alabama in the Senate. On March 12, 1946, identical bills were introduced in both houses of Congress. Two years later, after Senator George Aiken of Vermont joined Hill in sponsoring the bill, the demonstration bill passed the Senate on the unanimous consent calendar on February 28, 1948. Despite a favorable report by a House subcommittee, however, no action was taken by the House in 1948.

The pattern of progress of library bills in the Senate and lack of progress in the House continued for two more years. Amid high hopes among librarians, the bill actually got to the floor of the House in the Eighty-first Congress after it was reported favorably by the House Education and Labor Committee, and received a rule from the Rules Committee. The House debated H.R. 874 for five hours on March 9, 1950, but the librarians and their supporters were scarcely prepared for the result. The bill was defeated by a vote of 161 in favor, 164 opposed.

In the perspective of history one can only be amazed that librarians came this close to passage of a major piece of federal legislation after only four years of work. Opposition to federal aid was still very strong in 1950. Moreover, the floor debate indicated strong resistance to aid for rural libraries. Even Congressman John F. Kennedy of Massachusetts questioned the wisdom of spending federal dollars for what was a "rural library program."

Yet the effect of the defeat upon the library community was devastating. Congressman Carl Elliott of Alabama (elected in 1948) and Bessie Moore, Arkansas Library Commission Chairwoman, confirm that judgment. As Moore notes,

> The library community just simply reeled from a knock-out. And it takes time to recover, time to re-think and organize. . . . Also, communities and more people became interested in libraries at this time. Some had counted on this [aid] to help and there was no help coming because the bill didn't pass.

The blow was even greater because everybody thought the bill was assured of easy passage in 1950. The Truman administration had supported it. Commissioner Earl McGrath of the Office of Education arranged meetings with various ALA groups and state librarians to discuss establishment of adequate library services in areas without libraries. Ralph Dunbar talked with librarians about developing plans for handling those glorious federal dollars soon to be pouring forth from Washington, D.C.

Nonetheless there were forces other than the traditional opposition to federal aid which hindered the library cause. Not the least of these problems was the turmoil in ALA when its long-time Executive Secretary, Carl Milam, resigned, and the pressure on ALA finances became acute. Milam's successor, John Cory, notified Paul Howard in June 1949, that the Washington Office would be closed in the fall because the Library Development Fund had been depleted. Howard then resigned to become Librarian of the Department of the Interior on August 1, 1949. While Cory and another ALA staff member spent August 1949 in Washington, working for the bill, and while Mrs. Aubrey Lee Graham agreed to operate a Washington Office out of her home, on a part-time basis effective October 1, these events resulted in a loss of momentum to say nothing of the loss of experience and background.

Howard's resignation triggered immediate calls for re-examination of the Cory decision. Ralph Lindquist, Chair of the Federal Relations Committee, suggested a compromise plan for funding the Washington Office.

On November 8, 1949, he proposed a $15,000 annual budget, which included $5,000 from the ALA operational budget, $5,000 from the ALA endowment (previously invaded for other purposes), and $5,000 to be raised among state library associations and individuals. The Washington Office was saved, albeit with some loss of momentum, and Marjorie Malmberg became its second director on January 1, 1950.

Would the Public Library Services Demonstration Bill have passed if these complications had not existed? No one knows. Certainly the absence of an experienced person in Washington during the crucial period before the vote must have had some negative effect. In any case, Paul Howard and John Lorenz agree that passage of the demonstration bill in 1950 might not have been in the long-term best interest of libraries. State library agencies were weak, and, in some states, nonexistent. Plans were not ready for spending the money. The library community itself was uncertain about the basic thrust of the bill. The Howard-Lorenz interpretation, of course, comes from the luxury of three decades of reflection. For those who had worked so hard and so long for this legislation, the March 9, 1950 defeat was a stunning blow.

Chapter 3

The Library Services Act Emerges (1950-56)

Recoiling from the 1950 defeat, supporters of a federal program for library development both in Congress and in the American Library Association began work anew on library legislation. The Director of ALA's Washington Office, Marjorie Malmberg, (January 1, 1950-August 31, 1951) renewed efforts to work closely with legislative staffs of the Senate and House committees responsible for library bills. In developing new legislation she took into account the various points made by opponents in the House floor debates. Although we were not able to interview Marjorie Malmberg, Julia Bennett Armistead, her successor, gives Malmberg credit for laying the ground work for the brief interim period of Alice Dunlap (September 1, 1951-January 31, 1952) as well as Bennett's own successful tenure in that office (February 1, 1952-November 1, 1957). Julia Bennett Armistead has commented that the transformation of the library demonstration bill into the Library Services bill had been made before she joined the ALA Washington Office staff as an assistant on March 1, 1951. For that to have been accomplished within a year of a crushing legislative defeat seems truly remarkable. One is inclined to agree with Bessie Moore that six years to reorganize, rally the troops, and pass a major piece of legislation, indeed the *first* major piece of educational legislation since the Morrill land-grant acts and the G.I. bill, is not too long a period. It only seems interminable to those who are involved.

INFLUENCE OF THE SOUTHERN LIBRARIAN

Julia Bennett was a southerner. She started her library career in Knoxville, Tennessee and had worked as a reference librarian in Pasadena,

11

California and as Director of the Extension Department of the Charlotte-Mecklenburg County Public Library before coming to Washington to work for the ALA Washington Office. Some time after she was appointed, she learned that there were a number of people both in the book industry and the Association, who thought that it would be best for the Director to be a man. That view was not shared by ALA's new Executive Secretary, David Clift. Bennett attributed part of her success to the confidence and support Clift gave her.

One should remember that southern congressmen and senators dominated the congressional committee power structures in the fifties. By being re-elected year after year, many had risen through the seniority system to key leadership positions. Carl Elliott recalled that at this time thirteen of the nineteen committee chairmen in the House were from the South.

Senator Lister Hill (Alabama), who became Chairman of the Senate Labor and Public Welfare Committee in 1950 and served until 1968, and Graham Barden (North Carolina), who was Chairman of the House Education and Labor Committee from 1952 through 1960, were crucial individuals because library legislation originated in their committees. Senator Hill, sponsor of the original demonstration bill in 1946, was an advocate for libraries throughout his long career in Congress.

Graham Barden, however, was the key person to be won over to support the Library Services Bill, because he controlled the House committee. A conservative southern Democrat, Barden had strong reservations about supporting an increased federal role in libraries and education. On the other hand, he had voted for the Library Demonstration Bill in 1950, and his wife had served as a public library trustee in Craven County, North Carolina. Barden, like some of his fellow chairmen, ruled his committee with an iron hand. His reluctance to appoint subcommittees and delegate legislation to other members of the committee meant that any library bill had to wait in line behind major labor and other federal aid to education legislation on the committee's agenda. Many attribute Julia Bennett's success to her ability to work closely with Graham Barden.

Carl Elliott described Julia Bennett as having been a very good personal politician. This, she says, is what she tried to be. In her six-year tenure in Washington she developed supportive working relationships with Senators Hill and Aiken, Graham Barden, Edith Green, Carl Elliott, John Fogarty, and other members of Congress and their staffs. Also of critical importance were the contacts she made with the legislative staffs of the key standing committees of Congress. Especially important among these individuals were Fred Hussey, Chief Clerk of Barden's House

Committee on Education and Labor; Stewart McClure, Staff Director for Hill's Senate Committee on Labor and Public Welfare; and John S. Forsythe, General Counsel for the House committee and later for the Senate committee.

Emerson Greenaway described how Julia Bennett (and her successors) educated the library community so that they became effective politicians on the national level. Crucial to their success was the knowledge of where to go within the federal bureaucracy, among congressional staff members, and with other national groups headquartered in Washington for the help needed to pass library legislation. The fifties provided a training period for librarians to learn the political facts of life. They learned how to identify important constituents of key congressmen and to communicate effectively with them when action was needed on the library bill.

The importance of the southern delegation in Congress meant mobilizing the state librarians, trustees, and federal relations coordinators from the southern states so they could influence their representatives. Bessie Moore provided a vital link with the Arkansas delegation which included among others, Wilbur Mills, Chairman of the House Ways and Means Committee, Congressman Brooks Hays, Judge James Trimble of the House Rules Committee, and Senator J. William Fulbright.

State librarians in the South provided essential support. Evelyn Day Mullen, who at the time of passage of the bill was State Librarian of Alabama, provided a vital link with the Alabama delegation. In the 1950 debates, House opponents of the bill had said that no states had asked for a library bill. Mullen secured a resolution from the Alabama State Legislature in support of the Library Services bill. Elizabeth Hughey Arline, then State Librarian of North Carolina, provided an important link to Graham Barden. Lura Currier in Mississippi, Lucille Nix in Georgia, Essae M. Culver and Sally Farrell in Louisiana, and countless other southern librarians, trustees, and laypersons worked closely with congressional leadership from the South.

THE NATIONWIDE EFFORT

Important as the southerners were, they were by no means alone. Support for national programs had to come from all sections of the country. Since the focus was on rural library service programs, the smaller rural states were also crucial. Julia Bennett worked well with librarians and congressional leaders from all parts of the country. To promote the ALA legislative network she visited many state and regional association meetings.

Early in her tenure as director, Julia Bennett went north to acquaint herself with the members of the New England Library Association. While there she also made a tour of the New England state libraries. She was surprised upon her visit to Montpelier, Vermont, to be greeted at the railroad station not only by the state librarian but also by Senator George Aiken with whom she soon developed a close personal working relationship. George Aiken, along with Senator Irving Ives of New York, had won many Republican supporters to the bill by the time it passed in 1956.

Another of her major tasks was coordination of effort. The ALA Washington Office was located in the old Congressional Hotel. It became the communications hub for the national effort. Located across the street from the House Office Building on New Jersey Avenue, the Congressional Hotel proved an admirable site for Julia Bennett and her secretary, Lois Nuse, to carry on their work. Here they kept in touch with the field by phone and correspondence, and held meetings with key library and congressional leaders and staff. They printed the *ALA Washington Newsletter* on a mimeograph machine located in a former dressing room. It was a very functional arrangement. Julia Bennett and/or others could spend the night there if late-breaking congressional action made it necessary.

The director's activities included annual and midwinter meetings of the ALA Federal Relations Committee and frequent contacts with state federal relations coordinators and state librarians. With her knowledge, optimism, and charm, she converted many doubters within the Association, who did not think that federal legislation would ever be successful. According to Bennett, at a special time of discouragement, "I kept saying that we were going to make it in this particular Congress in the summer of 1955."

In her own interviews Julia Bennett emphasized that ALA leadership on the national level came from all types of libraries, not just public libraries, and, as Emerson Greenaway noted, not just from librarians serving rural areas. John Ottemiller, Associate Director of the Yale University Libraries, was the Chairman of the ALA Federal Relations Committee for the critical years for LSA of 1952/53 through 1955/56. Roger McDonough, State Librarian of New Jersey, succeeded Ottemiller in 1956/57, served through 1959/60 and was followed in turn by Emerson Greenaway from 1960/61 to 1965/66. After 1960 the ALA Federal Relations Committee became the "ALA Committee on Legislation."

Ottemiller was a hard worker. Even though he was an academic librarian whose major interests were government documents, postal rates, and the Library of Congress, Ottemiller strongly supported the Library Services bill. He presided over an ALA Federal Relations Committee of fifteen to seventeen members. The size of the committee is perhaps indicative of the interest and effort ALA exerted for passage of the bill.

Julia Bennett also stressed the importance of federal relations coordinators in each of the states. Some of the most active people in support of the Library Services bill were heads of the larger public libraries and academic and research libraries. They saw the need for the legislation, even though it did not affect them directly. Edmon Low, an academic librarian from Oklahoma, and later a member and chair of the Legislation Committee was one of these early federal relations coordinators. Germaine Krettek, a public library director from Iowa, was a federal relations coordinator for that state before becoming Director of the Washington Office herself in 1957.

Bessie Moore has noted the coming together of a lot of different forces in the mid-fifties for support of libraries. She remembered particularly the revival of the trustees group in ALA. These individuals not only had valuable political contacts but they were also perceived as concerned citizens, without the vested interests of librarians or representatives of the book industry. Moore recalled the good work of persons like Ruth Berg of Indiana, Alice Wallace of Massachusetts, and Frank Milligan of Iowa.

The Washington Office also provided the base from which Bennett could keep up continuous contacts with various national organizations and federal agencies headquartered in Washington. These contacts were important in winning support for the Library Services Act. Among the groups with whom Bennett worked closely were the National Congress of Parents and Teachers, American Council on Education, General Federation of Women's Clubs, and National Education Association. These groups later participated in the hearings held before congressional committees and supported the cause of libraries.

SELLING THE LIBRARY SERVICES ACT

As has already been indicated, experience with the library demonstration bill enabled the supporters to write new legislation which took into account some of the objections of their opponents. Paul Howard had already found help, if not support, from the unlikely office of Senator Taft. The congressional allies and their friends produced a new bill with several major differences from the demonstration bill. There was greater flexibility in state use of funds, a definite maximum of $7.5 million per year in the authorization, adoption of a variable matching formula in distributing funds, and provision for expansion of programs as funds and personnel became available. Still, the Library Services bill was intended to stimulate states and localities to provide library services to rural areas, or more precisely, those areas of 10,000 and under in population. There was an almost naive belief that, once library service could be demonstrated to citizens, they would demand that it be continued.

On May 1, 1951, Senators Aiken, Hill, and Paul Douglas introduced the new Library Services bill and on August 16-17, 1951, eight congressmen introduced identical library bills in the House. A Senate committee reported the bill favorably on September 17, 1951, and a House subcommittee reported it favorably to the full Committee on Education and Labor in April, 1952. There it languished for the next three years. Meanwhile, the librarians gathered their forces. David Clift became Executive Director of ALA in 1952 and began a push that enabled Ed Low to call the next two decades "a raising of the federal consciousness about libraries."

The early fifties were truly a missionary period for extending public library service to the unserved, according to John Lorenz. In agreeing with Lorenz, Roger McDonough recalled that his predecessor as head of the New Jersey Public Library Commission had the title "Secretary and Missionary," which he inherited in spirit. Said McDonough, "I always loved that and I never discounted the title, because there is a lot of missionary spirit in those of us who have been engaged in selling library service."

When asked what was the chief motivation for passage of the original Library Services Act, Congressman Elliott responded, "that it lay in the increased awareness of people in general that libraries and information should be available to all of the people. World War II had had a great leveling influence and had increased this awareness of the need for information for everyone." Elliott thought library service for all rooted itself in the basic democratic ideals of Thomas Jefferson. Freedom of information is needed by a literate public in order to govern itself. He emphasized as well that absence of books and libraries in rural areas was particularly felt by their inhabitants and by many of his colleagues in Congress. Rural public library service had great appeal to congressmen, most notably Speaker of the House Sam Rayburn, Carl Perkins of Kentucky, and members of Congress from the Plains States and the West. They recalled growing up in rural areas without having access to books and libraries. They believed that delivery of books to rural areas would diminish the sense of loneliness and isolation among young people and adults, bring intellectual stimulation, relieve boredom, and enhance and enrich the lives of people in rural areas. Besides, the citizens of cities, and most notably, the populous areas of New England, the Middle West, and Middle Atlantic states, already had libraries. It was only fair that library service be provided to rural citizens as well, even if it meant federal action to encourage the states and localities to provide it.

Extension of library services to rural areas also paralleled the major social movements affecting rural areas that had begun in the 1920s and 1930s. Paul Howard, who had begun his career as a librarian in the thirties in Oklahoma, linked rural library service to the development of Rural Free Delivery mail service, agricultural extension and demonstration, the building of rural roads, rural electrification, and the "Sears Roebuck Catalog."

Evelyn Day Mullen recalled the work of the famous North Carolina Home Demonstration Director, Jane McKinnon, who referred to the Tarheel State as being full of "growing edges." Many of the southern states had passed state library aid legislation in the early 1940s but the problem in North Carolina, which was not unlike that in many other states, was that they either had county library systems or no libraries at all.

> We felt like we needed, and most of us felt like there was a place where, federal aid could help us over some of the areas where we had no local funds that we could count on. We had state aid but it could only go so far. The federal aid would help these growing edges that we had to build on. We were ready for it because we had state-wide plans in the Southeastern states.

As a part of their missionary efforts in the early 1950s, librarians produced statistical evidence of the need and introduced it into the arguments made before Congress. Paul Howard had testified before the Senate Committee on Labor and Public Welfare in 1946 that there were 35,000,000 persons out of a total population of 132 million without any library service. By 1950, library statistics showed that less than 63 percent of the people in the country lived where library service was available. Of that number 88 percent lived in rural areas.

Senator Lister Hill testified before a House subcommittee in 1952, that there were 33 million people, mostly living on farms and in small communities, without library service; an additional 35 million people with inadequate library service; 600 counties, or one in five in the country, without any public library service; and that less than one-third of the nation's 3,070 counties had county-wide service. Further, Senator Hill argued that public library service supplemented and complemented the public school system. Such service was needed for students for home study and for adults to continue their education.

One of the key tools in extension of public library service to rural areas, which had great appeal to congressmen, was the bookmobile. When Carl Milam, the ALA Executive Director in 1944, had talked about the rural library demonstration bill to Paul Howard, he had said he wanted a library bill with "sex appeal" for congressmen, something that would catch their attention. It was the popularity of the bookmobile service, noted Howard, that provided that appeal.

John Lorenz emphasized the drama in bringing books to rural areas via bookmobiles. He added that the bookmobile was not a phony concept, and it did provide an opportunity for a congressman to have his picture taken in front of the bookmobile. What the bookmobile really did was to open a new world to rural people. Many statements in the record show what bookmobiles meant to communities and schools as they provided books for the first time. Lorenz has never forgotten the statement of the rural lady getting off the bookmobile, coming back to the door, and shouting, "Hiram, come here quick. We're rich, we're rich."

Politically, the bookmobile played a role in the passage of LSA. Paul Howard recalled Nancy Gray of North Carolina bringing her bookmobile to Washington and Graham Barden recessing a meeting of his committee so he and the other members could look at it.

Julia Bennett Armistead believes that Carl Elliott was the first congressman to take a ride through his rural district on a bookmobile. He and Evelyn Day Mullen took this trip together in 1955. Later Elliott used this example in his testimony before the House hearings on LSA and on the House floor debate for its passage.

Eileen Cooke noted that even to this day, Congressman Carl Perkins, who came to Congress in 1948, remembers vividly bookmobiles going into the mountains of Eastern Kentucky and providing his constituents with library services for the first time.

OVERCOMING POLITICAL OBSTACLES

In the 1950s several thorny issues faced anyone attempting to get new federal education legislation through Congress, and especially through the House of Representatives. These issues were so formidable that no other major aid to education legislation passed Congress until the National Defense Education Act was passed in 1958, two years after the Library Services Act.

The substance and exact wording of the library legislation developed in its ten-year evolution since 1946 were designed to overcome these issues and obstacles. To promote the bill in Congress, Julia Bennett showed political astuteness. Her activities during this period included: (1) securing sponsors for the bills in Congress; (2) mobilizing support from the library profession and lay leaders for the library cause; (3) careful preparation in advancing the legislation through each step of the law-making process in Congress; (4) selection and preparation of appropriate witnesses to testify before congressional committees; and (5) exercising sensitivity in dealing with individual members of Congress.

Lobbyist Charlie Lee describes the political obstacles as "The Three Reefs, which sank many an education bill—Religion, Race, and Radicalism." Fortunately, he says, solutions to these issues were found for the library bill that allowed it to pass eventually with only minor difficulties.

The religious issue was tied to the constitutional problem of giving educational aid to parochial schools. The Library Services bill surmounted this obstacle because public libraries served all citizens whether they attended public or private schools.

The race issue was just beginning to build up momentum in Congress and was linked in the minds of most southern congressmen with the concept of states' rights and a corresponding reluctance to support legislation that appeared to have any potential for federal control over state activities. From the very beginning the Library Services bill had incorporated language which said that determination of the types of services to be offered, the books to be purchased, and the plan to be followed in spending any federal money allocated to the states would be left to the states themselves. John Richards, testifying before the House Education and Labor Committee in 1955, assured the committee that the bill would not have any affect on the issue of integration versus segregation. Charlie Lee notes also that difficulties inherent in this issue were cleared out of the path of the library bills by the Senate Commerce Committee which enacted a Civil Rights Act, a law of general applicability, that defused race as an issue in relation to the Library Services bills. The radicalism issue was more an issue of the sixties.

Lorenz and Bennett disagreed somewhat with Charlie Lee on the relative importance of these issues to passage of the library bill in 1955-56. They believe that the issue of federal control, in the sense of libraries being considered state and local responsibilities, remained the most formidable issue they faced. Lorenz stressed the fact that, in many states, public libraries were not yet considered state responsibilities and the large majority of states did not yet have state aid provisions for public libraries. Moreover, Julia Bennett recalled that in the Eighty-second Congress, around 1953, the Intergovernmental Relations Study was undertaken. The task of the Kestnbaum Study, as it is also called, was to identify all of the various departments, subdepartments, commissions, and other bodies of the federal government, and their responsibilities. It was her opinion that it would have been impossible to get the Library Services Act through at that time.

The issue that later caused the library community the most difficulty however, was whether the Library Services Act should be viewed as a temporary measure. Was it a one-time, five-year-long demonstration, after which the states and localities would have been sufficiently stimulated to accept responsibility for public libraries? In the beginning, the bill was viewed as a temporary measure.

In effect, in their naiveté the librarians said to Congress, "If you pass this bill, we will not be back." John Richards, ALA President, 1955-56, told Congress as much in his 1955 testimony. This "one-shot" approach was generally the position of many members of the American Library Association. They expected the $7.5 million each year for five years ($37.5 million over the entire period) to solve all the problems of rural public library service. That approach came back to haunt the ALA when it became clear that the first four years had not accomplished all that had been envisioned, and therefore an extension would be necessary.

Behind the scenes Julia Bennett had to deal with these major issues on a daily basis. She also had to take into account a number of minor issues in advancing the legislation and in knowing when to act. To assist her she had many congressional allies. By the 1956 session when the bill finally passed, there were eighteen sponsors in the Senate and twenty-seven sponsors in the House. One should remember that the bill had started its progress in 1946 with one sponsor in the Senate and one in the House. Even with this growing support, there were still many ways opponents could have blocked the bill. Moreover, as Chairman of the House Committee on Education and Labor, Graham Barden had, in effect, life-and-death control over the library bill.

Julia Bennett Armistead commented

> Graham Barden was really the key as far as I was concerned, with getting the bill through. There were others—Carl Elliott, Phil Landrum, Lee Metcalf, and they all played an important part in the House Committee. But without the nod from Graham Barden we would have gotten nowhere. He could certainly pigeonhole a bill if he wanted to. . . . He also influenced other members, particularly of the Southern delegation, who might have been on the fence and indecisive. When they saw him, who had been a leader in the opposition to federal aid to education, take the stands that he did, it played a part in influencing other members.

She relied on Barden's judgment in maneuvering the bill through Congress and worked with him through the three Congresses with which she was involved, the Eighty-second, Eighty-third, and Eighty-fourth. He advised her when it was time to act.

In 1955, when it came time to appoint the subcommittee that would hear testimony on the library bill, Barden asked Bennett to suggest the names of the members she would like to have. She asked for the three

Democrats who were later to serve on the subcommittee, Edith Green, Phil Landrum, and Lee Metcalf. She had also asked for Carl Elliott, but Barden told her Elliott had other assignments. In requesting two Republicans, Bennett suggested Albert Bosch of New York and Peter Frelinghuysen of New Jersey, who would be favorable to the bill. Barden accepted her suggestions and appointed them, saying she had picked some of the best people on his committee.

However, the ranking Republican member, Samuel McConnell of Pennsylvania, did not go along with Barden's suggested appointments. He insisted on appointing two freshman Republicans as counterparts to Edith Green in Oregon (Sam Coon) and to Lee Metcalf in Montana (Orvin Fjare). McConnell did not want to see a unanimous subcommittee report on the bill and assured that outcome with his appointments. Julia Bennett thought that very unfair. She knew going into the House hearings that the final vote would be 3 to 2. She noted that Fjare did not even attend the hearings.

Barden appointed Phil Landrum of Georgia as chairman. The four Democrats decided that they would allow Edith Green's name to be placed upon the bill. As a first-term congresswoman from Oregon, Green would pull off a coup in having a bill pass under her name. Bennett, at the time, felt that this was a mistake and that the bill would be stronger with Landrum's name on it.

THE HOUSE HEARINGS, 1955

The year 1955, therefore, seemed appropriate for a major effort at passing LSA. Many regard the House Education and Labor Committee hearings on May 25, 26, 27, 1955, as the crucial dates in making a strong legislative case for the Library Services bill. These hearings received wide publicity in the library press, with the *Wilson Library Bulletin* providing extensive coverage in its September 1955 issue.

An impressive array of thirty-seven witnesses, including ten members of Congress, appeared before the subcommittee. John Richards, the President of the American Library Association, 1955-56, noted that 27 million people lacked public library service, that 404 counties did not have public libraries, and that only in the states of Delaware, Massachusetts, and Rhode Island did public library service reach every citizen. Further, he cited the ALA standard of $1.50 per capita as the amount needed to render even minimum library service and the fact that, of the 7,500 public library systems in the country, 77 percent had budgets of less than $10,000. He also emphasized that LSA was to be a temporary act, a point many opponents remembered four years later. As expected, the subcommittee voted 3 to 2 in favor of sending the bill to the full committee.

Considerable time elapsed between the hearings in late May and committee approval by a 20 to 9 vote in July, 1955. However, Congress recessed in the fall without acting on the bill. Nonetheless, Bennett reassured her library colleagues that 1956 would be the year the bill *would* pass. In April, 1956, Chairman Barden got the House Rules Committee to give the library bill a favorable rule to provide for two-and-one-half hours of debate on the floor of the House of Representatives.

Not one to leave anything to chance, Bennett, with the help of Ralph Dunbar, prepared a notebook filled with all of the questions they thought might be asked in the course of the debate. They reviewed all the questions that had been raised in the hearings, tried to come up with answers to these, and tried to anticipate other objections which might be raised. "Julia's notebook" had thirty to forty pages with an index and cross-references.

Bennett also worked with supportive congressmen who assigned specific colleagues to handle certain questions on the floor. An example was Lee Metcalf of Montana, a lawyer respected on both sides of the aisle, who was responsible for answering any questions that might come up regarding civil rights and the library bill. Copies of the notebook were reproduced for sponsors of the bill and other key members.

The librarians and their allies were well prepared for their next crucial battle, the House debate on May 8, 1956. Graham Barden as Chairman of the Committee on Education and Labor and Phil Landrum, who had chaired the subcommittee, sat at one of the two tables in the front of the House floor. Edith Green sat close to the front but not at the table with Barden and Landrum. Congressman McConnell handled the minority view from the other side.

The House floor debate opened auspiciously when Representative Bill Colmer (D-Mississippi) expressed his suppport, "I do want to say at the outset that it is a bill that I have been conclusively sold upon." Lura Currier, State Librarian of Mississippi, had done her job of lobbying for the library bill very well indeed. Colmer then recognized Representative Howard Baker, Sr. (R-Tennessee) who spoke in favor of the bill. Even before the bill had been given over to its sponsors to handle the debate, these two strong statements assured the bill both bi-partisan and conservative southern congressmen's support.

Barden and Landrum spoke for the bill and assured the members that there was nothing in the bill that linked it to public school education, nor would the bill violate the principles of states' rights and responsibilities. Representative Thomas Pelly (R-Washington) asked if there were any provisions in the bill to assure that the funds would not be used to bring about racial discrimination or segregation. Lee Metcalf, as planned, fielded the question and assured the gentleman from Washington that the bill had nothing whatsoever to do with the issue of segregation. Edith Green, the bill's sponsor, spoke briefly and said, "It is true the bill has my name on it, but because so many of these members have worked on it far longer than I, it could well be called the Carl Elliott bill, the Phil Landrum bill, the Thomas Jenkins bill, or the Frank Smith bill." She told them further that the per capita cost attached to operation of the bill would amount to the price of "a five-cent piece of chewing gum." There was no response to her statement. A number of other objections were raised and handled. After the two and one-half hours of debate the bill passed on a voice vote.

In the gallery were Julia Bennett, David Clift, Nettie Taylor, a group of high school students who had appeared at the House subcommittee hearings, and other interested librarians and trustees. The anxiety level among the supporters was high as each question was asked and they noted the response and the outcome. From time to time Graham Barden looked up into the gallery to indicate to Bennett how things were going. That evening after the bill had passed on a voice vote, he was to remark to her, "You were really sweating it out up there, weren't you?"

With success at last assured in the House, Senator Hill acted immediately to move the bill forward in the Senate. On June 6, 1956, the Senate approved the Library Services Act on a unanimous vote and sent it forward for President Dwight D. Eisenhower's signature. Eisenhower signed the bill on June 19, 1956, at the same time that the American Library Association was holding its annual meeting in Miami Beach. The assembled librarians responded to this news with cheers. Charlie Lee noted that librarians were always at a summer conference when important legislation was pending in Congress!

Librarians celebrated their success by making Senator Lister Hill an honorary member of ALA. Acknowledging the key role of Julia Bennett in LSA's passage, Bessie Moore headed a spontaneous effort to raise funds for purchase of a diamond wrist watch. After she presented the watch to a surprised Julia Bennett, conference exhibitors added a $500 bond for "Miss Library of Capitol Hill." Euphoria resigned supreme.

Chapter 4

Implementation of LSA: Appropriations and Administration (1956-60)

Earlier we mentioned that Paul Howard and John Lorenz doubted that librarians were ready for federal funds for libraries in 1950. Were they better prepared in 1956? Probably, but not without a further struggle. After the ebullient celebration in Miami in June 1956, they still had two major obstacles to overcome before they could enjoy the benefits of their hard-fought victory. The first, of course, was an appropriations battle. Librarians had to learn the hard way that *authorizations* by the Congress rarely equalled *appropriations*. So their first task was to secure the $7.5 million which P.L. 597 authorized. The second, even more hidden obstacle, was interpretation of the law by government attorneys and the establishment of an administrative framework for approval of state plans for disbursing the funds. To these two obstacles the librarians and their allies had to turn their attention upon their return from the Miami conference celebration.

THE STRUGGLE FOR APPROPRIATIONS

The Library Services Act established an authorization level of $7.5 million per year for five years. With that amount of money, the library community expected to overcome years of neglect and lack of development of library services in rural areas throughout the country.

In her enthusiasm, Julia Bennett thought surely the appropriations committees in the House and Senate would provide the whole amount

25

authorized. The Commissioner of Education had requested $7.5 million plus $140,000 for federal administration. Besides, there was so much support for the bill in Congress. However, even though the commissioner requested the full amount for LSA, the Bureau of the Budget first reduced the amounts requested and then restored them. Ominously, President Eisenhower's message concerning appropriations for LSA contained the following statement:

> Less than the full authorization under Public Law 597 is recommended because it is necessary to build up an administrative staff in the Office of Education and the States must take steps to prepare State plans and establish eligibility for Federal grants.

The budget request reached Congress on July 20, 1956, but was too late to be considered by the House Appropriations Committee, the normal procedure. Since the request also went directly to the Senate on the same day, it was considered first by the Senate. ALA President Ralph Shaw and Harold Tucker, Librarian of the Queens Borough Public Library (Jamaica, New York), represented the American Library Association before the Senate Appropriations Committee where they requested the full amount of the authorization. On July 21, the Senate committee reported out the bill with a recommendation for appropriation of the full amount of $7.5 million. On July 25, the Senate passed its appropriations bill with the LSA full amount intact, a remarkable achievement, even in an election year. So far everything was going according to schedule.

The conference on the Second Supplemental Appropriations bill between the House and Senate lasted for two hours on July 26, 1956. House conferees balked at appropriating the full amount for LSA as recommended by the Senate. The Conference Committee then reduced the appropriations for the first year to $2,050,000. Actually, librarians were more fortunate than they knew. Appropriations for some other programs added by the Senate, which had not been approved by the House before the conference, lost their entire appropriations. In their two-hour meeting, the House and Senate conferees had to resolve a diffence of $453,458,038—the total amount added to the appropriations bill by the Senate. Librarians won their $2 million; some other groups lost. Nonetheless, to Julia Bennett the hopes of the library community seemed dashed again. In recalling the occasion Roger McDonough said,

> She was desolated, truly. I was serving as a consultant to Ralph Dunbar, then Head of the Library Services Bureau. We were sitting there working on the very begin-

nings of the regulations to the Act and the telephone rang. It was Julia calling us from the Washington Office. She was literally in tears.

In her strained voice she told us how instead of $7.5 million the Act had authorized we would get only $2,050,000. She said of her library peers, 'I've let you down.' We had to comfort her.

I said, 'Julia, you haven't let us down. You have an Act passed and signed into law and it took years and years to do it. This is a major breakthrough. The initial money is much less important than the authorization and the fact that we are now able to move.'

Graham Barden also comforted Bennett about the low appropriations. "Now, Julia, quit worrying about that because you couldn't use $7.5 million dollars if you got it today."

In retrospect Bennett feels that Barden was correct. A small amount was needed to get started. It would have been worse to have had the money and not to have been able to spend it properly. It was better to start small and build up.

REGULATIONS AND ADMINISTRATION

Putting the Library Services Act into operation required translation of the statute into administrative procedures, rules and regulations. This process took nearly six months, from June 19, 1956, when the law was signed, until December 6, 1956, when the final rules and regulations were printed in the *Federal Register*.

On July 1, 1956, Roger McDonough began work as a consultant with Ralph Dunbar and the legal staff of the Department of Health, Education, and Welfare in developing the rules, regulations, and administrative procedures for the Act. Also at this time John Lorenz, then Assistant Librarian of the Michigan State Library, became a consultant to Dunbar. In addition, Isabel DuBois, formerly director of Navy libraries, worked with them in preparing the rules and regulations. Their counterparts in the task of interpreting the law and drafting rules and regulations from the Office of Legal Counsel of the Department of Health, Education, and Welfare were Joseph H. Meyers, Assistant General Counsel, Harry J. Chernock, and David S. Seeley.

To librarians, developing the regulations was a part of their continuing education. Few had much knowledge of the legal process in implementing legislation. As John Lorenz noted, librarians had much to learn about dealing with a group of lawyers who insisted on examining the meaning of every word in the Act. The word that gave the lawyers the most trouble was "extension," "the extension and development of library services." Their original interpretation was that this meant that the states and localities must come up with matching money, above and beyond any existing money that had been appropriated. Lorenz tried to convince the lawyers that in writing the legislation, the intent was to use the professional meaning of "extension," that is, you extend service to parts of a state that previously had no services. Struggles between lawyers and librarians over the interpretation of the language of the Act went on for months.

The federal government began communicating with the states about the Library Services Act in August, 1956. U.S. Commissioner of Education, Samuel Brownell, wrote the governors of the states to announce the enactment of the Library Services Act and ask for information about the official state library extension agencies. Two states, Arizona and Utah, did not have such agencies when LSA was enacted. On August 15, 1956, the first funds from LSA were made available to the Library Services Branch.

In September two representatives from each state library agency were invited to attend one of four regional conferences on the legal problems involved in administering LSA on the federal and state levels. The Library Services Branch, its consultants, and the Office of Legal Counsel developed three documents which were used as the basis for the discussions at these regional meetings. These were: (1) "Tentative Draft of Rules and Regulations," (2) "Guide for Submitting State Plan," and (3) "Forms for Use in Submitting State Plan."

The first meeting was held September 20-22, 1956, in Washington, D.C., and included representatives from fourteen states from New England and the Atlantic Coast, as well as Indiana, Ohio, and Michigan. A second meeting followed in Nashville, Tennessee, on September 27-29 for ten Southeastern states. The meeting in Sacramento, California, on October 11-13 was attended by representatives from eleven Western states and the territories of Alaska and Hawaii. A final meeting in Kansas City, Missouri, on October 29-31 included all the rest: North and South Dakota, Nebraska, Kansas, Oklahoma, Texas, Minnesota, Iowa, Missouri, Arkansas, Illinois, Louisiana and Wisconsin.

Lorenz stressed that it was only after these four regional meetings that the Office of General Counsel was convinced that the only way the Act and its administration could get started was for them to interpret LSA in a way that did not require new and additional money on the part of the states and local communities. Beyond this, Lorenz noted that these initial regional conferences established an important precedent for communication between the federal agency and the state agencies that is useful to this day.

Elizabeth Hughey Arline, who in 1956 was the State Librarian of North

Carolina, remembered fussing and fuming about the proposed federal regulations at the Nashville meeting. However, she added that the regulations, which required that the state plan be reviewed with the governor, the state treasurer, and the attorney general, gave her and other state librarians an opportunity for a type of communication that previously they did not have. Thus, even without the full appropriation that first year, state librarians were able to accomplish a great deal in educating their respective state government officials about libraries.

On November 7, 1956, the Office of Legal Counsel agreed to revise their tentative regulations. On December 6, 1956, the final rules and regulations were published in the *Federal Register*, and copies were sent to the state library agencies. The initial administrative basis for the Library Services Act was complete.

STATE PLANS FOR LIBRARY DEVELOPMENT

Agreement on the aims, methods, and terms to be used in administering the Act was the principal outcome of the series of regional conferences. The state plan for library development, a comprehensive statement prepared by the state library agency, has remained the basic document. The planning process which the Library Services Act required of the state library extension agencies, as noted by Molz and other library observers, was one of the major contributions of the Act. It required the states (1) to formulate and describe their plans for library development, (2) to provide information on objectives and policies for the use of state, local, and federal funds for a five-year period, (3) to report on methods for administering their plans, standards to be used, and priorities to be set. For each year, every state was required to describe projects to be undertaken and a budget for each project.

The planning process required of the state library extension agencies had three basic components:

1. *A State Plan.* It was a comprehensive statement, submitted according to a specified outline and formulated by the authorized state library agency. The plan included such information as the legal authority of the state agency to carry out the state plan and the aims, policies, and methods of administering the plan for the five-year period. A state was allowed to amend its basic state plan at any time by submitting amendments for the approval of the U.S. Commissioner of Education.

2. *The Program of each State* was a document submitted annually which included a description of what the state agency intended to do with state, local, and federal funds during each fiscal year of the project and des-

ignated the rural areas of the state to be served. The program was subdivided into projects, each of which was described separately.

3. *The Budget* for projects for the fiscal year was ordered by categories of expenditure and showed all planned expenditures for which the state expected the federal government to pay the "federal share." The amount of the federal share ranged from 33 percent to 66 percent of the costs of the program depending upon the per capita income of the state. The categories of expenditure included salaries and wages, purchases of books and other library materials, purchase of equipment, and other operating expenses. No funds could be used to erect a building or purchase land for a library.

The basic *state plan* has continued to serve as the legal instrument between the federal government and the states, with some slight modification brought about by amendments to the Act. The *Federal Register* is the basic source for information about administration of the Act. However, regulations have been supplemented by interpretations on legal questions surrounding the administration of the Library Services Act and its successor, the Library Services and Construction Act, made from time to time by the Office of General Counsel of the Department of Health, Education, and Welfare. A numbered series of these various legal opinions has been maintained at the Department of Education since the Act's beginning in 1957.

The first state programs under the Library Services Act got underway in early 1957. By January 25, 1957, the Library Services Division had approved 8 of the 22 state plans. By March 29, 1957, 38 state plans had been received; 31 had received approval and their first Library Services Act funds.

In February, 1957, the Library Services Division, with John Lorenz, now the assistant director and responsible for LSA, added three library extension specialists to assist in the administration and support of the Act. They were Wilfrid F. Morin, formerly of the Extension Department of the New York State Library; Evelyn Day Mullen, formerly Director of the Library Services Division of Alabama; and Helen Luce, formerly Librarian, San Bernadino (California) Public Library. Rose Vainstein, formerly of the Gary (Indiana) Public Library, became the new Public Library Specialist.

The people, procedures, and programs envisioned by the promulgators of the Library Services Act were in place. Implementation could now begin, along with judgments about the Act's effectiveness in stimulating state and local support for rural public library programs. Were the librarians and their allies correct in their belief that federal funds would so demonstrate the value of library services that state and local funds would be provided to continue such programs when federal funds were no longer available?

APPROPRIATIONS FOR FISCAL 1958

In the Spring of 1957, Julia Bennett led ALA's first campaign for full funding for the Library Services Act. On February 28, 1957, she began a practice that her successors in the ALA Washington Office would follow. She testified before the House Appropriations Subcommittee when it considered the budget for the Department of Health, Education, and Welfare. A friendly chairman, John Fogarty, Democratic congressman from Rhode Island, welcomed her appearance. Fogarty proved to be a staunch advocate of federal library appropriations until his death in 1967.

Lukewarm support from the administration was reflected in a request by the President and Secretary of HEW for only $3 million for LSA in the fiscal 1958 budget. In her testimony to the House Subcommittee, Bennett argued for the full amount of the authorization—$7.5 milion. On March 29, 1957, the House voted an appropriation of $5 million for LSA, $2 million more than the amount requested by the president. In the House floor debate on March 29, 1957, Representative Hiestad (R-California) offered an amendment to cut the $5 million to the president's recommended figure of $3 million. After an hour of debate his amendment was defeated by a vote of 94 to 71.

In an economy conscious Congress, the Library Services Act program received the only increase over the administration's proposed budget for the entire Health, Education, and Welfare Department appropriation. Congressman Fogarty led the debate and strongly supported the LSA increase. Over twenty representatives from all over the country spoke for the $5 million and against the Hiestad Amendment. Many others were prepared to speak if there had been a need to prolong the debate.

At the Senate Appropriations Hearings on April 11, 1957, Marion Folsom, HEW Secretary, spoke against the House recommendation of $5 million for LSA. He cited the fact that his department had recommended a $1 million increase for the program but that a $2 million increase beyond that would "advance this program disproportionately to many other important and needed programs." On May 7, Julia Bennett testified for full funding of LSA and received support for her request from the National Education Association, National Congress of Parents and Teachers, and Senators Arthur V. Watkins (R-Utah) and

Henry Jackson (D-Washington). On June 12, 1957, the Senate voted to uphold the $5 million for the Library Services Act as passed in the House. One important provision was added in the Senate, which would allow any funds not matched by a state to be redistributed and made available to other states.

No conference action was necessary this time since the amounts in both houses were identical. President Eisenhower signed the appropriations bill on June 29, 1957. By August 12, 1957, funds for LSA were released by the Bureau of the Budget and could be sent to states whose 1958 plans had been approved. A small delay had occurred when Percival Brundage, Director of the Bureau of Budget, sent a letter to the heads of all departments asking them to hold their spending for 1958 to the 1957 level. This would have been disastrous for LSA which had received $2,050,000, all of which had been spent in the last half of the previous fiscal year. In releasing the funds, the Bureau of the Budget specified that the LSA payments be released in two payments, $2.5 million in August and $2.5 million in January, 1958. Through the efforts of many senators and representatives interested in the library program, LSA funds were released on schedule and further delays were avoided.

JULIA BENNETT LEAVES THE ALA WASHINGTON OFFICE

Enthusiasm for the new federal library legislation was high in the summer of 1957. Success of the $5 million appropriation for 1957-58 seemed assured. Ralph Dunbar and John Lorenz had written an article, "Uncle Sam Befriends Libraries," for the June 22, 1957, issue of *Saturday Review*, which also published other items on LSA. Clearly, there was strong public approval for the new legislation.

Amid this enthusiasm there was a dark cloud approaching on the horizon. Julia Bennett announced that she would leave the ALA Washington Office to be married to John M. Armistead, a Knoxville, Tennessee, attorney in the fall. Bessie Moore remembered her reaction to Bennett's resignation "I remember my reaction when Julia left. I thought the world had come to an end. I just wondered how we were ever going to mobilize [without her]." Bennett had been a key figure in the revival of the library bill and her departure signaled a major loss for the profession.

At the ALA Conference in Kansas City, June 23-29, 1957, there were many testimonials to her good work, including a council resolution introduced by Roger McDonough for the Federal Relations Committee expressing "appreciation for a magnificent accomplishment in Washington, [and] . . . [describing] what a pleasure it has been to work with her in our common pursuit of the goals of American librarianship and that it wished for her every possible happiness in the years ahead." ALA's appreciative words would be re-echoed by numerous congressmen and senators as well as officials of other educational organizations before Julia Bennett's departure from the Washington Office on October 31, 1957.

Moore's world had not really come to an end. Bennett's successor, Germaine Krettek, was equally dedicated and competent. *Time* magazine would eventually label her one of the most effective lobbyists on Capitol Hill. Bessie Moore concurred with this judgment. She had originally thought ALA "couldn't *possibly* have gotten anybody that would do the job as well as Julia did." When she heard that the Association had succeeded in attracting Krettek as Bennett's successor she felt "Germaine would just be great . . . and I was never disappointed. . . . The ALA Legislation Committee reached its zenith under the leadership of Emerson [Greenaway] and Germaine because they made such a wonderful tactical team."

Krettek, then Director of the Council Bluffs, Iowa, Public Library, assumed her duties as Director of the ALA Washington Office on November 1, 1957, and served until her retirement on November 30, 1972.

INITIAL STATE PROGRAMS UNDER LSA

The first funds for LSA did not reach the states until January, 1957. Since states had six months or less to develop state plans and get programs underway, those states which had made plans in anticipation of LSA's passage were fortunate. In a series of four reports in the late fifties, the Library Services Branch summarized the initial activities spawned by LSA. The basic report, *State Plans under the Library Services Act; A Summary of Plans and Programs for Fiscal 1957* . . . (1958), and three supplements covering the years 1958, 1957-59, and 1957-61, the USOE documents record LSA's accomplishments during its first five years both in narrative and statistical form. An early problem area was the length of time required for successful development of library projects under LSA. That problem provided ammunition for the librarians in the battle for LSA's extension in 1960.

Yet documentation of the Act's success is impressive. During its first year of operation, fiscal 1957 (July 1, 1956, through June 30, 1957), thirty-five states and one territory (Hawaii) submitted state plans and programs which USOE approved. In the following year forty-five states and five territories participated.

Notably absent in 1957 and 1958 were the states of Delaware, Indiana, and Wyoming. Indiana and Wyoming subsequently certified that they would not request LSA funds, and so their allocations were made available to other states, including Arkansas.

Bessie Moore noted with satisfaction a speech she made in Indiana where she expressed her appreciation to her audience: "Thank you for helping us [Arkansas] get new bookmobiles. I am so glad you didn't take your money." The governor of Indiana had stated in newspaper headlines, "He didn't want Hoosiers brainwashed by books selected by federal bureaucrats." The strong language in the Act assuring state control of the funds had had no effect on him. In fact the law stated,

> The provisions of the act shall not be construed as to interfere with State and local initiatives and responsibility in conduct of public library services. The administration of public libraries, the selection of personnel and library books and materials, and, insofar as consistent with the purposes of the act, the determination of the best uses of the funds provided under the act, are reserved to the States and their local subdivisions.

Nonetheless Indiana's governor remained adamant. Indiana did not participate in the federal library services program until March 1, 1961, when it became the last state to join the program.

The whole aim of the federal legislation was to stimulate state and local support for rural public libraries. Rural areas were defined as any place of 10,000 population or less according to the latest U.S. Census. By 1960, the Library Services Branch reported impressive results for the first three years of operation. Thirty million persons in rural areas had new public library services available to them for the first time. State funds for development of rural public library service had increased by 54 percent since 1956. Local appropriations for rural public libraries were up 45 percent. Sixty-five rural counties and an equal number of New England towns, formerly without public libraries, had library services for the first time. Finally, the major effort in the states was the demonstration and development of county and regional library systems, many of them served by more than 200 bookmobiles placed in operation under LSA projects.

On a broader level, the Office of Education reported three other accomplishments of the Library Services Act which can be considered major influences on the direction of public library development:

> 1. Basic strengthening of the resources and services of state library extension agencies.
> 2. A comprehensive pattern of professional and nonprofessional library training activities.
> 3. The creation of a new and enlarged concept by a vast number of people of

the role which a good public library can play in the life of every citizen. (*State Plans under the Library Services Act, Supplement 3. A Progress Report, The first Five Years. Fiscal 1957-61*, pp. 1-2).

As enthusiastic reports of the use of Library Services Act funds by the states reached Washington, the annual appropriations battle in Congress toward achieving the full amount authorized for LSA became somewhat easier. The $5 million appropriated in fiscal 1958 was increased to $6 million in 1959 and to the full $7.5 million for both 1960 and 1961.

Chapter 5

Battle for Renewal of the Library Services Act (1960)

A sense of urgency pervaded the library community during the initial five-year life of the Library Services Act. John Lorenz noted that a great deal of fervor and energy was exhibited in those early days. This paid off in Congress where LSA gained a reputation for professionalism in administration. Congressmen recognized LSA as a program that was being administered with enthusiasm and creativity, which had produced results. They therefore supported it. Bennett emphasized that LSA was a great hit with Congress, because after the money was distributed, librarians could report back what was being done, what kind of plan each state had, what other states were doing, and how the money was being used. Because of earlier fears about federal control of libraries, the lack of restrictive federal regulations and the encouragement for each state to develop its own plan and use the methods that worked best for each state meant a great deal to congressmen who followed the progress of the Act. Many congressmen reported to Bennett that they felt that "the nickels and dimes of the program were being used to the fullest extent."

Firmly fixed in the minds of all those involved with LSA was the termination date of the Act set for June 30, 1961. Many librarians within the ALA and opponents of the rural library legislation in Congress recalled John Richards's testimony to the effect that the librarians would not be back at the end of five years asking for an extension. Yet it was clear that the optimism of Richards and others was unfounded. Consequently the dominating issue for the library community in 1960 was the survival and continuation of the Library Services Act.

37

LEGISLATIVE INITIATIVES IN 1959

Roger McDonough, then Chairman of the ALA Federal Relations Committee, introduced a resolution to support the extension of LSA at the January, 1959, ALA Council meeting. Admitting that their own earlier optimism had created a problem, McDonough nonetheless felt ALA had a good rationale in asking for renewal. He pointed out that several factors had worked against successful implementation of LSA in the allotted time: (l) It took longer to get started than anticipated — to get rules and regulations written, to get the lawyers in USOE to interpret the law as those who had worked for LSA all those years were certain it was meant to be interpreted, and to get staffs organized. (2) The states didn't come through as anticipated because there was a lot of selling to do, and also because so many of them were on biennial budget cycles and there were only two legislative sessions in that first five-year period. (3) Finally, the full authorization of $7.5 million per year had not been appropriated. The ALA resolution provided spirited discussion but was finally approved by a comfortable margin.

Germaine Krettek, who had replaced Julia Bennett as ALA Washington Office Director on November 1, 1957, emphasized that it did not take long to realize that towns of under 10,000 population were not going to be able to fulfill their responsibilities to all the citizens in rural areas. They needed to be able to depend on the larger public libraries so that the total library resources of an area could be made available. In time, this realization led to an emphasis upon regional development and interlibrary cooperation.

During the spring of 1959, at congressional appropriation hearings, both Senator Lister Hill and Congressman Fogarty inquired about the extension of LSA. Senator Hill said, "Certainly the success of the program up to date and the fact that the program has been only partly carried out, as contemplated, would strongly suggest that the Act should be extended."

Congressman Fogarty stated, "I think we are running a really good program and hope that we can see this expanded and not take a step backward, as this budget indicates. I think there is still a great need. Have you given any consideration to the extension of the legislation yet?" Librarians and their allies obviously had considered the need for extension. They were not long in finding a champion for their cause.

On January 6, 1960, on the first day of the second session of the Eighty-sixth Congress, Carl Elliott filed the first bill to extend the Act for five years after it expired in 1961. Elliott called for the same level of appropriations of $7.5 million annually. As Chairman of the Special Education Subcommittee of the House Education and Labor Committee he would have responsibility for the bill in the House where it would face its most difficult test. By the end of the Spring, 1960, fifty-two persons had submitted additional bills in the House in support of the extension of the Library Services Act. Meanwhile in the Senate, Lister Hill and fifty-two cosponsors introduced S. 2830, a bill to extend LSA for an additional five years.

The LSA extension bill had to be brought up in 1960, if funds for the Library Services Act were to be included in the president's budget when it was presented to the Eighty-seventh Congress. Otherwise, a new bill would have to be introduced and passed early in that session so that an appropriation bill could be passed before the June 30, 1961 termination date, a risky business at best.

Within the American Library Association, members discussed a number of amendments to broaden the scope of the Library Services Act. In fact, one resolution had already been introduced in Congress by William Green of Pennsylvania in August, 1957. House Resolution 402 would have authorized the Committee on Education and Labor to "study the problems of providing adequate public library services in our metropolitan areas, including services which transcend State jurisdictions, with particular reference to the management, support and use of the metropolitan library units." Green's resolution was referred to the House Rules Committee where it died peacefully.

Congressional insiders advised against amending the Act in 1960. In an election year any amendments should be held until after the national party conventions are held in the summer. The supporters anticipated congressional consideration only for noncontroversial matters. Thus the prospects for a simple extension seemed the most promising approach.

Librarians, while aware of the difficulties, were heartened by their congressional allies. Too, in his budget message, President Eisenhower for the first time had recommended full funding for LSA. In the House hearings held on March 29, and April 6 and 7, 1960, there was great support for extending the Act. On May 12, 1960, the full House Education and Labor Committee under Chairman Graham Barden voted out a "clean" bill to extend LSA for five years at the same authorization level and sent the bill to the House Rules Committee. On May 26, 1960, the Senate approved the extension of LSA without a dissenting vote. All seemed in order, despite reminders by some congressmen that the librarians had assured them they would not be back.

THE HOUSE RULES COMMITTEE REFUSES TO GIVE LSA A RULE

On June 2, 1960, Carl Elliott appeared before the House Rules Committee to ask for a rule so that the extension bill could be brought to the House floor. The Rules Committee denied the request, on a tie vote, as it was later determined. Chairman Howard Smith (D-Virginia) and William Colmer (D-Mississippi) had joined four Republicans to block passage of the bill. In the light of such formidable opposition there seemed little prospect that this vote could be overturned.

Congressman Elliott remembered that session before the Rules Committee vividly,

> It fell my lot to carry the bill to the House Rules Committee in the Summer of 1960. Everybody wanted to talk at once about what had been promised to the Rules Committee in 1956. They said, and these were fellows who used that as an issue at home, saving money and balancing the budget, and fiscal responsibility,all that kind of business. They made speeches about how irresponsible we were. We had brought them a bill that said it would cure all library ills and now, even before the bill expired, before we had even seen if the ills could be cured, we were back begging again. They said, 'No, we won't do that.'

Elliott sought out Clarence Brown (R-Ohio), member of the Rules Committee and someone a great deal more conservative than he, but someone whose word he trusted. He told Brown, who represented a rural district in Ohio and owned a number of small rural newspapers, "Clarence, there can't be anything wrong with a bill that brings information to farm families. You have made your living bringing information to those same families."

Brown replied, "Of course, there isn't anything wrong with it. It's just the method that you all have used. I want to help you. You know we all have to say things to keep our record straight." Brown had already made a speech castigating the library supporters for their irresponsibility and for coming back so soon and for so much.

Still he told Elliott, "If you will go back to your committee and get them to report out a bill for $3 million in authorizations for each year, I'll be glad to help you with it. I'll help get it out of the Rules Committee."

Elliott talked to many supporters of the extension of the Library Services Act about Brown's proposal. He thought to himself, "If we agree to that, and I don't say that the proposition was not made in good faith, then library services will be dead for all time for sure if we cut it from $7.5 million to $3 million a year. If we run our string out with $3 million then we are finished." So Elliott turned down Brown's proposal but not before he saw another way to solve the problem.

SAM RAYBURN AND THE MOTION TO SUSPEND THE RULES

Elliott had been speaking with House Speaker Sam Rayburn for some time about the merits of the rural-oriented Library Services bill. This struck a responsive chord with Rayburn who recalled the loneliness he experienced growing up in rural Tennessee and rural Texas. Elliott shared the same background, having grown up in rural northwest Alabama.

Throughout their discussions Rayburn and Elliott evolved the idea that one of the ways to break down that rural isolation was to have books available to people, to rural people. After a number of conversations, Elliott says that Rayburn told him, "I am going to recognize you to suspend the rules when we have a suspension day, when we get back here in a couple of weeks. And we will pass that bill."

A motion to suspend the rules under the procedures of the U.S. House of Representatives was a difficult parliamentary maneuver. First, it could only be entertained on the first and third Mondays of each month, and it required the approval of the Speaker. Before being submitted to the House the motion had to be seconded by a majority of the members. The proposition under consideration was debated for forty minutes, twenty minutes by those in favor and twenty minutes by those in opposition. Finally, to pass a bill brought up under suspension there must be a quorum of members present — 219 members — and passage required a two-thirds majority of members voting.

Elliott approved Speaker Rayburn's proposal. "That pleases me very much but to get two-thirds of a vote for any proposition is awfully hard. We must be sure."

"What I was trying to do," said Elliott, "was to get him to take as much responsibility as possible to get everybody there, see that they voted, and see that they voted right where he could affect the outcome." Rayburn responded affirmatively.

On 5:30 A.M. on Sunday, July 3, 1960, just before the House recessed, Germaine Krettek remembered, John Fogarty obtained the consent of Speaker Rayburn to call up the library extension bill under Suspension of the Rules on August 22, 1960.

LOBBYING FOR THE EXTENSION OF LSA IN THE SUMMER OF 1960

From the time Congress recessed on July 3 until it reconvened on August 15, the library community had six weeks to rally support for the extension bill. Action was taken on several fronts, most notably, at the national party conventions, which had met in July and had selected as their presidential candidates, John F. Kennedy and Richard M. Nixon. Both would lend their support to the extension of the Library Services Act. Elliott and Krettek recalled how this came about.

According to Elliott,

> We got John F. Kennedy to give us a categorical statement that if he was elected president, and if a library services bill was passed or anything close to it, or akin to it, and he made it pretty broad, that he would sign it. Not only that, he would support [it] in Congress and he would sign it.
>
> The effect of that, politically, was to say, in the midst of the campaign that was developing between Kennedy and Nixon, was to say to the Republicans, 'Now what do you say? It's your move next.'

Nixon also agreed to support the extension of the Library Services Act and issued a letter to that effect. As Congressman Carl Elliott noted:

> I think that did a great deal to quiet the normal opposition on the Republican side that would have come to our bill. If that opposition had gone to its full flower, Gerrie, we could not have gotten two-thirds of the vote. . . . Kennedy made his statement and he was good at that sort of thing. . . . Kennedy had a flair for things political. He had a flair for understanding them and had a great flair for how to use them. . . . He built the issues to Republicans by issuing statements in advance about things he would do. I have always thought that that helped to make up for the difference that we customarily had in the vote and allowed us to get the two-thirds.

Krettek added,

> Can I say that Mr. Elliott is not giving himself enough credit? I sat in his office when he talked to John Kennedy. When he got the commitment from Mr. Kennedy, he picked up the phone and called Mr. Nixon's office. He said that Mr. Kennedy was going to make this statement and asked what he was going to do. Carl parlayed the one against the other.

Another aspect of the fight to get the two-thirds vote for extending LSA came from Emerson Greenaway's representation of ALA at the platform hearings for each party. On June 3, in Salt Lake City, Greenaway testified before the Democratic Platform Committee, which was considering problems in education. Later he testified at the Republican Platform Committee meeting. This in itself was a notable accomplishment since few organizations were given the opportunity to present their views at these platform hearings.

The platform adopted by the Democratic National Convention meeting in Los Angeles on July 12, 1960 contained the following statement:

We pledge further federal support for all phases of vocational education for youth and adults; for libraries and adult education; for realizing the potential of educational television; and for exchange of students and teachers with other nations. (*ALA Washington Newsletter,* August 12, 1960).

On July 27, 1960, the Republican platform included this statement in its educational plank:

Toward the fullest possible educational opportunity for every American, we pledge these actions:
. . . Support of efforts to make adequate library facilities available to all our citizens.

Library observers noted that a library scene was also included in the Republican television platform presentation. (*ALA Washington Newsletter,* August 12, 1960).

KRETTEK AND CHAIRMAN BARDEN LOCK HORNS

Graham Barden, who had supported passage of LSA in 1956, was a congressman who took seriously the idea that the Library Services Act was to terminate in 1961. A conservative Democrat from North Carolina, Barden, said Krettek, "supported libraries but didn't want to spend any money on them." She had a difficult time with him in the Spring of 1960 but was successful in getting him to report the extension bill out of his committee and send it to the Rules Committee where it was stuck.

Krettek added, "All that Barden needed to do was to speak to Bill Colmer and Judge Smith on the Rules Committee and say that this was my bill and I want it out. It would have gotten out, but he wouldn't do that."

Barden was at home in North Carolina for the recess when the decision was made to circumvent the Rules Committee by bringing the extension bill up under suspension. However, Krettek kept in touch with Barden's legislative assistant, Fred Hussey, and told him everything the supporters of the bill were trying to do to get the bill passed.

When Barden returned after the recess, he called Krettek and was very angry,

Any time I want a bill out of the Rules Committee, I can get it out. You had no business doing this while I was out of town. He further stated that I hadn't played fair with him, that he didn't know what was going on. That if we had kept him properly informed that the bill would have been handled properly, and not in this fashion.

Krettek responded,

> Mr. Barden, this is not true in any sense of the word. . . . You are misinformed because you knew exactly what was going on because I talked to your administrative assistant, Fred Hussey, and gave him all the information each step of the way. You had every opportunity to bring the bill out. . . . We have to get this bill out and you are keeping us from getting it out.

After the vote, Barden called Krettek, "Gerrie, you've got real guts. You did exactly what you had to do under very difficult circumstances. . . . That's what it takes and you did exactly the right thing."

THE HOUSE FLOOR VOTE ON THE EXTENSION OF LSA, AUGUST 22, 1960

At twenty minutes to three on Monday afternoon, August 22, 1960, Carl Elliott, the Chairman of the Special Education Subcommittee of the House Education and Labor Committee, moved to suspend the rules and pass the bill to extend the Library Services Act for five years. Normally, the Chairman of the House Education and Labor Committee, Graham Barden, would have led the debate on a bill emanating from his committee. Elliott called up the version of the bill passed by the Senate, S. 2830, in lieu of H.R. 12125, which was bottled up in the Rules Committee. Barden walked to the back of the chamber and took a seat to watch the proceedings.

Elliott argued before the House that there were 40 million people yet unserved by public libraries. There had been many intangible benefits from passage of the original bill in 1956. The prestige of local and state library groups had been increased and they were working more actively than at any time in history. A tremendous amount of public interest in libraries had been developed and there was a much greater degree of cooperation among libraries all along the line from the local to the national level. To the objection that extending the Act was unnecessary because the job had been accomplished, Elliott argued that the job was only half done. One major reason was that Congress had not appropriated all of the $37.5 million authorized in the original bill.

Elliott cited support for the extension bill from U.S. Commissioner of Education, Lawrence Derthick, the members of his subcommittee, and from members of both parties. He noted that both party platforms supported the bill. Moreover, there were fifty-two cosponsors of the bill in the House. Elliott had a special message from the nominee of his party, John F. Kennedy, supporting the bill. In his letter of August 19 to Elliott, Senator Kennedy stated,

I should like to congratulate you on the magnificent fight you have made to assure the extension of the Library Services Act. I am confident that when the House acts under a suspension of the rules on August 22 the bill will be passed. As you know, I have long had a similar interest in the extension of this act, and supported it both in committee and when it passed the Senate. . . . The program is an important asset to our Nation. It helps provide both recreation for our minds and strength and vitality for our human resources. (Text in Fry, "LSA and LSCA," p. 13).

Applause greeted Elliott's initial statement and revealed the temper of the House. Elliott then yielded the floor to Representative William Colmer (D-Mississippi) and member of the Rules Committee, who stated that reluctantly he couldn't vote for the bill without breaking faith with the House Rules Committee. They opposed the bill because they had been promised in 1956 that the bill would be for five years only. Frank Bow (R-Ohio) more actively opposed the consideration of the bill citing the promises that the original bill would last for only five years. He quoted his former colleague from Ohio, Cliff Clevenger, whose favorite saying was, "There is nothing so permanent in Washington as a temporary agency."

Nonetheless, there was strong support for extension from Representatives from both sides of the aisle and from all regions of the country. Vice-President Nixon's letter of support for extending LSA was presented by Congressman Stuyvesant Wainwright of New York. Nine other Republicans spoke in behalf of the bill or later submitted statements for the record.

Krettek summarized the opposition to the bill as revolving around the issue of federal aid to education and not about aid to libraries, the same argument used in 1950 and 1956. Many of the opponents of the bill noted that they were not against libraries and some even paid tribute to the job being done in their states under LSA.

Krettek and Lura Currier, the State Librarian of Mississippi, watched the proceedings from the gallery, as guests of House doorkeeper, William M. "Fishbait" Miller. Lura Currier had worked with William Colmer throughout the years. Elliott paid tribute to the lobbying of the southern state librarians as some of the finest that he had ever seen. Nothing had been left to chance. In fact, Krettek had arranged with Miller to be sure the Library Services bill was placed in a strategic location on the Speaker's desk so that when he came to the bill, which was the third of six items on the agenda that afternoon, he would be sure to take it up during the time available.

One surprising and significant aspect of the opposition came when the vote was called by Speaker Rayburn. A few congressmen, who for reasons compelling to them, could not vote for the bill, quietly rose and walked out of the House chamber, including Barden and Colmer. Not voting against a bill, when an affirmative vote of two-thirds is required, was almost voting for the bill since one negative vote required two affirmative votes to offset it.

The final vote was 190 to 29 in favor of extending the Library Services Act. On August 31, 1960 President Eisenhower signed the bill which extended LSA until June 30, 1966.

Elliott concluded that it was at that time that he came to feel that "we had won our spurs. That library service was part of the permanent structure of the United States [government] . . . I think it still is."

Chapter 6

The Kennedy Years (1961-63)

The election of John F. Kennedy to the presidency in November, 1960, and control of both houses of Congress by the Democratic Party marked a turning point in the history of the Library Services Act. With four years of success for the Library Services Act under their belts, and the extension of the Act for five more years assured, the American Library Association was poised in 1961 for new initiatives in the area of federal aid to education and libraries. Librarians would succeed in securing federal support for libraries beyond their fondest dreams.

PRELUDE TO THE SIXTIES

In addition to LSA, which is the focus of this report, the American Library Association had been helpful in securing passage of the National Defense Education Act (NDEA) in 1958. This Act brought some federal aid to school and college libraries for the first time. While discussion of NDEA is obviously beyond the scope of this report, the role of the American Library Association and the efforts of Congressman Elliott and Senator Lister Hill, co-authors of the act, should be noted. Passage of NDEA paved the way for other education legislation which would constitute one of the legacies of the Kennedy administration.

NDEA was the first omnibus education bill to pass Congress after many years of effort. In large part the passage of the act was due to public reaction to the Russian launching of Sputnik and its presumed challenge to the scientific and technical prowess of the United States.

By linking educational legislation to the nation's military defense, the supporters of federal aid to education were able to use the Soviet threat to surmount the obstacles that had blocked federal aid to education legislation for years. The issues were the same ones librarians had to surmount in the fifties—the issues of integration and segregation of the races and the church-state issue which involved the constitutionality of providing federal aid to parochial and other private schools and institutions of higher education. These two issues continued to hinder passage of education legislation in the early months of the Kennedy administration.

School and college libraries benefitted under NDEA, which provided for the purchase of

> laboratory and other special equipment, including audio-visual materials and equipment and printed materials (other than textbooks), suitable for use in providing education in science, mathematics, or modern foreign language . . . and for minor remodeling of laboratory or other space used for such materials and equipment.

Roger McDonough believes the American Library Association was very influential in the passage of NDEA and possibly had more to do with its success than the National Education Association, a much larger organization, but, at the time, not in good standing on Capitol Hill.

Charlie Lee thought that Senator Lister Hill saw the opportunity to load NDEA with all the items that he and his colleagues had been trying to get through Congress for years—scholarships, fellowships, and loans; funds for testing and counseling programs, research and experimentation in the use of the news media like radio and television; and purchase of laboratory equipment and other materials, like library books, to improve instruction in the sciences and in foreign languages.

Lee agreed with McDonough about the political importance of ALA. Further, he maintained that the members and their staffs in Congress recognized that the American Library Association shared with certain other national organizations the status of "Locomotives." That is, ALA was an organization that could turn on the constituencies so that legislators could get a lot of "box cars" of their legislation attached to library legislation and pulled through the legislation process without any independent force behind them. Staffers recognized and also admired the ability of the ALA Washington Office to communicate instantly with the library community and ensure a prompt response when action was required on the Hill.

By 1961 the power of the appeal of libraries on the national level had begun to be heard and resulted in what is today called the "Golden Age of Library Legislation."

THE ALA COMMITTEE ON LEGISLATION IN THE 1960s

The ALA Committee on Legislation, formerly the Federal Relations Committee, was the focus for the legislative efforts of the Association.

From 1956-57 through 1959-60, Roger McDonough chaired the ALA Committee on Legislation. McDonough could be proud of the accomplishments during his tenure. The Library Services Act passed and had been successfully funded and extended. The National Defense Education Act had been passed and funded. The public relations program called "National Library Week" had been established in 1958. Libraries had been included in both party platforms in 1960. Within the Association McDonough had guided the development of the first comprehensive statement of the Association's legislative goals for all types of libraries. Finally, he had been successful in gaining bi-partisan support for library legislation during a time when there was a Republican administration under President Eisenhower, and the Democrats controlled both houses of Congress. McDonough and the members of his committee,[1] working closely with the ALA Washington Office, had laid the groundwork for the federal legislation which came to fruition under his successor, Emerson Greenaway.

Director of the Free Library of Philadelphia, Greenaway served as Chairman from 1960-61 to 1965-66. Greenaway seized the opportunity offered by the Kennedy administration. As already seen, the new administration was sympathetic to libraries. Further, Congress had shown itself to be supportive of libraries since the inception of LSA.

Bessie Moore contended that, "The political management of the Washington Office of the American Library Association came to complete fruition with the partnership of Emerson Greenaway as head of the Legislation Committee and Gerrie Krettek as Director of the ALA Washington Office. Now that was real political skill."

Emerson Greenaway would be the first person to tell you that he was not alone in this successful effort. Similarly, Gerrie Krettek added, "Thousands of people were involved—literally thousands."

THE MEETING AT THE WHITE HOUSE

Under Greenaway's chairmanship, the committee continued the practice of having small delegations of ALA leaders meet regularly with key

---

[1]Edmon Low of Oklahoma, Virginia McJenkins of Georgia, John Eastlick of Colorado, and Elizabeth Hughey of North Carolina in 1956-57.

government officials. These meetings were a technique for furthering the library cause in Washington. The one-on-one political interaction that these occasions created was well suited to the personal political skills of Greenaway and his committee. They proved most effective in achieving legislative results for libraries.

Members of ALA had, on many occasions, met with the U. S. Commissioners of Education. Also, they had met frequently with lower-level federal employees who occupied the strategic positions that lay between the Library Services Branch and the ever-shifting hierachy at the top. These meetings provided an important communications device in maintaining support for existing library programs and developing new legislative initiatives.

With the prospects for passage of a new, more comprehensive bill for libraries in the offing, the Committee on Legislation was concerned, as usual, with how to get their bill through Congress. Just prior to the Midwinter ALA meeting in 1962, Greenaway convened a small meeting on long-range planning to discuss legislative strategy.

In addition to members of the Legislation Committee and Krettek, the group included John Lorenz of the Library Services Branch, Ralph Dunbar, Paul Howard of the Department of Interior, Verner Clapp of the Library of Congress and Peter Muirhead and Ralph Flynt from the Office of Education. Also on board was a new committee member, Bessie Moore.

The two gentlemen from the Office of Education advised the group on techniques for getting the legislation passed. Greenaway remembered that Ralph Flynt had just told the group, "I never go to talk with anyone in authority without having a little schedule of something I want, just in case it comes up in the conversation. Then, I can reach in my pocket and pull out my notes and say this is a little draft of a plan I think has some importance."

Flynt was in the midst of his advice, said Greenaway, when there was a knock on the door of the small room in the Congressional Hotel where the group was meeting.

A gentleman came in and said he was Wilbur Mills and he wanted to speak with Mrs. Moore, if it wouldn't interrupt our meeting. So we looked at Bessie and she indicated that she would like to speak to Mr. Mills and off they went. After a while she came back and we got started again.

Then again there was another knock on the door. Brooks Hays came in and asked Mrs. Moore might he have a word with her? So Bessie had to get up and go out again. I wish you could have seen the faces of the two men from the Office of Education as they looked at one another. 'What goes on here?'

When the meeting resumed, Greenaway told the group, "I don't think we are going to get anywhere unless we get to the White House. There is no point in working our fool heads off unless we get the support of the President of the United States."

The meeting broke into small groups and Greenaway discussed how they might get an invitation to the White House. Verner Clapp interrupted him and said, "We have the answer right here in this room on our committee. I think that Bessie Moore could probably speak to one of her friends and get us an appointment."

Wilbur Mills was then Chairman of the powerful House Ways and Means Committee. Mrs. Moore had for years held an annual dinner for Mills in Little Rock. Brooks Hays, also from Arkansas, had just lost his bid for re-election to Congress and was an aide in the Kennedy White House.

Greenaway called Bessie down to their group and told her what the problem was. She told them she would have to make a couple of phone calls. In twenty minutes she returned and the ALA Committee on Legislation had its date with President Kennedy.

On March 20, 1962 members of the ALA Committee on Legislation went to the White House for their meeting with President Kennedy. Everyone was nervous about what was going to happen. First, the group waited outside in a large reception room. "Fishbait" Miller came out of an office and saw Krettek. He invited the group into a smaller office known as the "Fish" room, because of the pictures of fish in it.

Greenaway said, "I don't think the Legislative Committee has ever met in the White House so let us convene a meeting. We did and talked about our respective responsibilities when we met with the president. Then to our great disappointment we found that the president couldn't meet with us."

President Kennedy had been called away to meet with an ambassador, who was making an unscheduled stop at Andrews Air Force Base. Instead of President Kennedy, the library contingent was heard by two of his top aides, Ted Sorenson and Mike Feldman.

In the middle of Greenaway's sales pitch for libraries and the importance of supporting them, he was interrupted by Sorenson. "Dr. Greenaway, you don't need to convince us that libraries are important. This administration thinks so. Tell us what you would really like."

Both Sorenson and Feldman were great supporters of libraries. Feldman told Greenaway that as a boy he used to go to the library every week on his bicycle. The bike had a carrier on the front of it. He would go back home with it full of books from the library. Feldman, Greenaway learned, was from Philadelphia and knew all about the re-organization of the Free Library of Philadelphia, and the support Greenaway had from the Democratic mayor there. He was filled with admiration for the library.

Krettek had told the group not to come in laden with briefcases. However, Bessie Moore reached into her coat and pulled out a sheet of paper. It was a map of Arkansas and she had colored in the two or three counties with county library service. The remainder of the counties were just a big white area. "If this bill is passed," Moore stated, "then all these people that have never had library service will have library service." She then elaborated on the kinds of services that could be attained. Because she had been Chairwoman of the Arkansas Library Commission for so many years she knew the state very well and she had done her homework. It was very effective.

Just before the meeting was about to end and the outlines of the kind of bill they wanted the president to support had been drawn up, Greenaway was asked by Sorenson, "Now what do you want?"

Greenaway had not discussed what he was about to say to Sorenson with the Legislation Committee but he, too, had come prepared.

> Mr. Sorenson, you know if we have all these libraries, we have got to have a place to put the books, we are going to have to have a place for story hours for children and adult programs and to relate this all to good books and good reading. I think we need some money in this bill for construction of library buildings or the enlargement of the present buildings where there may happen to be a library building in a town.

Greenaway shocked Bessie Moore who thought "Emerson has ruined us. He has lost his cotton picking mind. [But] It got into the law." At that instant the idea of the Library Services and Constuction Act was born.

Within a decade the Library Services and Construction Act would provide funds virtually to rebuild the nation's public libraries, all on the basis of this inspired suggestion of Greenaway who had never discussed the idea with his committee.

MOVES TO EXPAND AID TO ALL LIBRARIES

A number of events had led up to the White House meeting. They are indicative of how the Library Services Act gradually took shape. President Kennedy's first budget request in January, 1961, called for the full $7.5 million authorized for the Library Services Act. In addition, ALA sought successfully to have a supplemental appropriation add $1,369,000 in the fiscal year 1960 to bring that year's funding up from $6,131,000, which had been appropriated, to the $7.5 million authorization. One reason for doing this was that the extension did not allow a carryover of funds from year to year.

On August 2, 1962, the House passed the fiscal year 1962 appropriations for the Labor-Health, Education, and Welfare Department budget and included the $7.5 million recommended by the president. In addition, House Report 392 which accompanied the bill contained praise for the success of LSA. It stated that since the start of the program over 6 million books had been purchased, over 100 rural counties had been aided, and LSA had been a fine demonstration of federal leadership in stimulating state and local effort. Since LSA's beginning in 1956, state funds for rural public library development had increased 75 percent and local appropriations 50 percent.

Finally, the report concluded with the following statement,

> While significant gains have been achieved there is still a big job which remains to be done in the whole field of library services. The committee was rather disappointed to find that the Office of Education is not giving more attention to the study and assessment of the deficiencies that still exist.

To assure closer attention to library needs, Congress appropriated an additional $50,000 in the fiscal 1962 bill to be used for three new staff positions for the Library Services Branch.

By 1962, the American Library Association's legislative program focused on implementing "ALA Goals for Action." The earliest efforts to change the Library Services Act envisioned an omnibus bill to provide federal aid for all types of libraries. Introduced to the ALA Council at the Midwinter, 1962 meeting, the new legislative program, "Goals for Action," aimed at a national program of library development. Training of librarians was also included as an essential part.

"The program should move ahead simultaneously on all fronts in order to achieve cooperative and interrelated development which is so necessary to accomplish the best use of library resources and services," the ambitious program stated.

Specific legislative goals were included for public, school, and academic libraries as well as for library education. Three changes in the Library Services Act were recommended:

1. Remove the 10,000 population limit and extend the public library development program to all population groups. The Association added the caveat that "It may be necessary to do this by steps."
2. Increase proportionally the authorization of $7.5 million to $20 million annually.

3. Change the expiration date of the Act from June 30, 1966 to June 30, 1968, and the "floor years" for state and local expenditures from 1956 to 1961. (*ALA Washington Newletter*, April 16, 1962, pp. 1-2).

For school libraries, "Goals for Action" called for an expansion of Part A of Title X of the National Defense Education Act, provision of matching grants to state educational agencies for establishing and maintaining school libraries, and federal grants of $30 million annually for five years terminating June 30, 1968.

For academic libraries, enactment of legislation based upon Part C of Title X of NDEA was sought in the amount of $10 million annually for five years. For library education, ALA sought grants for scholarships, traineeships, fellowships, short-term and regular session training institutes at the level of $7.5 million the first year, and $10 million for each of the next four years.

On March 27, 1962, Congressman Fogarty's House Subcommittee on Appropriations reported out LSA appropriations at the $7.5 million level. Again, the House Appropriations Committee report (H. R. 1488) praised the program and urged extending LSA to urban areas. On May 21, 1962, Representative Cleveland Bailey (D.-West Virginia) Chairman of the House Subcommittee on Education, introduced H.R. 11823, a comprehensive bill to amend the Library Services Act.

Carl Elliott, who previously chaired this subcommittee, had been requested by President Kennedy, Speaker Sam Rayburn, and other Democratic leaders to take a position on the newly expanded House Rules Committee. The Rules Committee had been expanded in 1961, when the Eighty-seventh Congress was organized, in an effort to insure that President Kennedy's legislative program would not be stymied in the House by an obstructive Rules Committee. Elliott's position on the Rules Committee proved important in getting the new bills for libraries through the House in 1963.

Congressman Bailey's bill included most points of the ALA legislative proposal and included federal aid for all types of libraries. By July 2, 1962, nineteen representatives from fifteen states had introduced identical bills.

On June 26, 27, and 29, 1962, the Subcommittee on Education of the House Education and Labor Committee held hearings on Bailey's and other related bills. The committee questioned many witnesses sharply on the possibility that under an expanded bill, rural public library service would be neglected by state library agencies. Additional questions referred to the purchase of religious books with public funds in relation to the June 25, 1962, Supreme Court ruling against official prayers in public schools. Could federal funds be used to purchase books on religion for public libraries?

Of special significance was the testimony of Wilbur Cohen, Assistant Secretary for Legislation in the Department of Health, Education, and Welfare, and Sterling McMurrin, the U. S. Commissioner of Education. Cohen maintained that "it is clear that additional federal assistance for library programs is necessary," but that

> In the limited time available since the introduction of these bills we have not reached a conclusion as to the exact scope and character of the provisions that should be included in an expanded Library Services Act, nor the exact size of the appropriations required to fund an adequate program. (*ALA Washington Newsletter*, July 3, 1962, p. 1).

On August 8, 1962, the House Subcommittee on Education reported favorably on an amended Library Services Act and sent it to the full House Education and Labor Committee. In an effort to encourage the House to pass the amended LSA, Senator Claiborne Pell of Rhode Island introduced an identical bill in the Senate. However, no further action was taken during that session of Congress.

On December 13, 1962, the *Wall Street Journal* speculated that President Kennedy "probably will endorse most features of an American Library Association proposal which calls for five-year expenditures of $310 million dollars." The article stated further, "Some strategists think a library bill, which appears to draw support from conservative Congressmen usually hostile to federal education aid, is an ideal vehicle for providing some help to elementary and secondary schools." The Library Services Act was, indeed, being viewed as Charlie Lee's "Locomotive."

The newspaper reporter who made these observations may have been the same one to whom Krettek referred. She remembered having her picture taken with President Kennedy.

> He brought into the White House all the heads of education agencies in Washington, and I was one of them. . . . This included the National Education Association, the American Council on Education, the American Vocational Association, the Catholic Library Association, and so on. I can remember we were sitting out in the anteroom waiting to go in. One of the reporters looked around the group and said, 'There goes the President's education program bill.' That meant that the Library Services bill was going to be included in the program.

Race and federal aid to education were dominant issues in 1962. The *ALA Washington Newsletter* reported that the congressional elections in 1962 were difficult for all members of the House Education and Labor

Committee because of the political burden of the issues surrounding federal aid to education. In fact, Cleveland Bailey, who had proposed the amended LSA legislation was defeated in his race in West Virginia. Three other members of his Education Subcommittee also left the committee for other reasons. In addition, in late 1962, a number of key members of the House Education and Labor Committee were said to be looking for safer committee assignments in the upcoming session. The fall of 1962 was marked also by a turnover in the top leadership of the executive department responsible for libraries. On November 14, 1962, an ALA delegation met with Anthony J. Celebrezze, the new Secretary of Health, Education, and Welfare, who had replaced Abraham Ribicoff, who had been elected to the Senate from Connecticut. On December 10, 1962, Krettek had the honor of representing ALA at the swearing-in ceremonies for the new U.S. Commissioner of Education, Francis Keppel, former Dean of the Faculty of Education at Harvard University, who had replaced Sterling McMurrin.

ROGER MCDONOUGH'S SURVEY OF LIBRARY SERVICES ACT ACTIVITIES IN THE SOUTH—1962

The Civil Rights movement in the South was moving-from the stage of freedom riders on buses traveling into the South, towards the massive confrontation of Martin Luther King and his followers with the Birmingham Police Chief "Bull" Connor in May, 1963. During this stressful period, U.S. Commissioner of Education Sterling McMurrin engaged Roger McDonough to conduct a confidential survey of LSA activities in the South. McDonough's job was to determine if LSA funds were being used to support and further the cause of segregation.

John Lorenz, then Director of the Library Services Branch, recalled that he and McDonough began talking about the study in the late fifties. The study was to be essentially one of fact finding, to determine what was going on at the state level in the South in terms of moving towards integrated library services. It was a question of finding out whether or not the library grants were moving in the right direction. Lorenz believes that McDonough's study, which was never published, put to rest the fears of the Office of Education that perhaps these funds were being used to further segregation.

McDonough met to map out procedures and ground rules with the state librarians for five southern states at the 1962 ALA conference in Miami Beach. He planned visits to Florida, Georgia, South Carolina, Mississippi and Louisiana, McDonough observed varying patterns of segregation and integration on a town-by-town, state-by-state basis. In some towns a common drinking fountain existed along with segregated toilets; in others the situation would be completely reversed. In New Orleans, McDonough remembered that the librarian of the public library, Jerome Cushman, integrated the water fountains by gradually lowering a huge oil painting until it covered the signs for separate drinking fountains!

During his visit to Mississippi, McDonough remembers being dropped off at night on a side street in a small county seat near Jackson by Lura Currier, State Librarian. There he met for two hours with leaders from the black community and talked about problems in providing library services in a segregated society. The blacks told him they had made tremendous progress and were getting help for their libraries from the state. McDonough had only admiration for the work of southern state librarians, like Lura Currier, who were doing their best to provide service to everyone under extremely trying circumstances.

In Georgia a top state education official told him, "We are watching the library program with keen interest. You are making progress that we in the school field did not think possible. We are sorry we are not moving as fast as you are but you are being our bellwether."

McDonough was embarrassed to see that Louisiana still had red and blue bookmobiles, one color for blacks and the other for whites. Even so, he noted, "To go out on a little country lane and see that bookmobile come down and sit by a church and have kid after kid walk down those dusty roads to borrow books was a thrilling experience."

When he met with Commissioner McMurrin, McDonough reported,

> that although there was some segregation going on, the majority of the white librarians administering the programs were doing their best within the constraints of local law and custom. . . . Some of them, like Lura Currier, were going beyond the call of duty. . . . The social gains that were being made far outweighed any little things that weren't happening. Overall, the sense of improvement was paramount.

LSA BECOMES LSCA

Because of the favorable administration response, the library community awaited eagerly the opening of the Eighty-eighth Congress, which convened on January 9, 1963. They were not disappointed. First, the president's budget request to Congress contained the following statement regarding his intentions in the field of education:

> A key objective of the coordinated program being proposed is to strengthen the quality of instruction and subject matter taught in our schools through (a) buttressing of research in education and improvement of course content, (b) expansion and

improvement of teacher training programs, and (c) improvement of community library services for people of all ages, and (d) strengthening of public elementary and secondary education.

In the Appendix was the statement: "As a part of the President's education program, reflected under proposed legislation, all public libraries will be eligible for Federal assistance, including construction."

In addition, the budget message also promised funds for college libraries (*ALA Washington Newsletter*, January 28, 1963, p. 1). Opponents of federal library legislation within the administration in 1963, most notably Walter Heller and other members of the President's Council of Economic Advisors, reportedly saw libraries as "bottomless pits" into which money could be poured endlessly and thus a field in which the federal government should not attempt to provide funds. However, on Tuesday, January 29, 1963, President Kennedy sent to Congress a special message on education. The administration measure was entitled the National Educational Improvement Act of 1963.

Throughout the President's Special Education Message and his proposed legislation, libraries were mentioned prominently. It was the first time that a major program of federal library legislation had been introduced under administration sponsorship and was therefore a tremendous breakthrough for libraries. President Kennedy's message began:

> Education is the keystone in the arch of freedom and progress. . . . For the individual, the doors to the schoolhouse, to the library and to the college lead to the richest treasures of our open society.
> . . . We must give special attention to increasing the opportunities and incentives for all Americans to develop their talents to the utmost—to complete their education and to continue their self-development throughout life.

Kennedy called for a program guided by a comprehensive approach to dealing with educational problems,

> An appraisal of the entire range of educational problems, viewing educational opportunities as a continuous lifelong process, starting with preschool training and extending through elementary and secondary schools, college, graduate education, vocational education, job training and retraining, adult education, and such general community educational resources as the public library.
> . . . Education cannot easily or wisely be divided into separate parts. . . . In order that its full relation to economic growth, to the new age of science, to the national security, and to human and institutional freedom may be analyzed in proper perspective, this bill should be considered as a whole, as a combination of elements designed to solve problems that have no single solutions.
> Education need not and should not end upon graduation at any level. An increasing number of Americans recognize the need and the value of continuing education.

... The public library is also an important resource for continuing education. But 18 million people in this nation still have no access to any local public library service and 110 million more have only inadequate service.

Advanced age, lack of space, and lack of modern equipment characterize American public library buildings in 1963. Their rate of replacement is barely noticeable: two per cent in a decade. There are now no Carnegie funds available for libraries—nor have there been for forty years.

The public library building is usually one of the oldest governmental structures in use in the community. In one prosperous midwestern State, for example, thirty per cent of all public library buildings were built before the year 1910, and 85 per cent were erected before 1920. Many other States are in a similar situation.

I recommend enactment of legislation to amend the Library Services Act by authorizing a three-year program of grants for urban as well as rural libraries and for construction as well as operation. (*ALA Washington Newsletter*, February 7, 1963, pp. 1-2, and Supplement).

In the House, Adam Clayton Powell (D-New York), Chairman of the House Education and Labor Committee, Carl Perkins (D-Kentucky), Edith Green (D-Oregon), James Roosevelt (D-California), and Carlton Sickles (D-Maryland) introduced identical bills containing the president's program. In the Senate, Wayne Morse (D-Oregon), Chairman of the Subcommittee on Education of the Senate Committee on Labor and Public Welfare, introduced an identical bill, along with the following cosponsors: Pat McNamara (D-Michigan), Ralph Yarborough (D-Texas), Joseph Clark (D-Pennsylvania), Jennings Randolph (D-West Virginia), Harrison Williams (D-New Jersey), Quentin Burdick (D-North Dakota), Claiborne Pell (D-Rhode Island), Mike Mansfield (D-Montana), and Hubert Humphrey (D-Minnesota).

On January 29, the morning the president's educational message was delivered, the ALA Committee on Legislation convened at the ALA Midwinter Meeting in Chicago. Emerson Greenaway discussed the provisions of the Education bill that the president would introduce that day. One problem that the committee had to address was the omission of major school library grants from the administration's bill. Cora Paul Bomar, State School Library Supervisor of the North Carolina Department of Public Instruction, expressed the concern of school librarians who had read the *Wall Street Journal* article of January 28, 1963, describing the proposed measure. The school librarians were fearful that granting funds to public libraries with special emphasis on their use by "students of all ages" might mean that this legislation would take the place of federal aid to school libraries. The committee was agreed that the intent of the public library aspects of the bill was to aid the development of public library services as such, distinct from any school library function. Also, the purpose of the administration in using this phrase in association with the legislation, said Greenaway, was to emphasize the educational role of the public library and encourage the purchase of serious reading rather than light recreational reading materials. The committee agreed that its report to ALA Council should make clear that the present legislation was not a substitute for needed aid to school libraries and that ALA would continue to give high priority to school library legislation. A point to be made, Greenaway said, was the need which the bill reemphasized for librarians, school administrators, college officials, and library trustees to develop overall state programs for library services to persons of all ages through the various types of libraries.

ALA school library legislation had been introduced into Congress in the form of an NDEA amendment by Congressman Elmer J. Holland (D-Pennsylvania). Greenaway also pointed out that, though it might not be meaningful at this time, it could be acted on if the political climate became propitious. The NDEA amendment concerning school libraries would die before May, 1963, however, a victim of the conflict generated by the church-state issues.

The Association of College and Research Libraries, Public Library Association, American Association of State Libraries, American Association of School Librarians, and the Council of the American Library Association all adopted resolutions in support of President Kennedy's proposed National Education Improvement Act at the ALA 1963 Midwinter Conference.

On February 4, 1963, the full House Education and Labor Committee, in an unusual fashion, began holding hearings on the president's education bill, H.R. 3000, rather than following the normal procedure of having subcommittees hold hearings on legislation before it was brought to the full committee. On February 8, 1963, Edmon Low, Librarian, Oklahoma State University and Vice President of ALA, represented ALA as part of a panel on the higher education aspects of the bill. James E. Bryan, President of ALA and Director, Newark Public Library, and Emerson Greenaway presented testimony on February 21 when Title VI, which included public libraries under Section C, was under consideration. In all, during 1963, the ALA and its Washington Office were involved in preparation for seven hearings and numerous other statements for the record.

On April 9 and 10, 1963, Congressman John H. Dent (D-Pennsylvania) Chairman of the Select Subcommittee on Education of the House Education and Labor Committee held hearings on H.R. 4879 and similar bills related to the public library services and construction provisions of the president's bill, H.R. 3000. Frances Keppel, U.S. Commissioner of Education, accompanied by Wilbur J. Cohen, Assistant Secretary for

Legislation of the Department of Health, Education, and Welfare testified on April 9 in support of Title VI, Part C. "The public library is a basic educational resource," stated the Commissioner. "The widespread recognition that education is a lifelong process has dramatized the importance of having good public library service readily accessible to every citizen. . . . Our national investment in good public library service is a direct and highly productive contribution to the intellectual life of our Nation."

On March 26, 1963, Germaine Krettek had appeared before the Labor-Health, Education, and Welfare Appropriations Subcommittee in support of the full $7.5 million authorized for the Library Services Act. On April 30, 1963, the full appropriation for the existing LSA for Fiscal 1964 passed the House.

Meanwhile, on April 24, 1963, the House Select Subcommittee approved by a split vote without amendment H.R. 4879, the public library services and construction legislation. The following day, Thursday, April 25, the full House Education and Labor Committee held an executive session to consider the bill but did not complete action. Thus the public library provisions of the president's omnibus bill became the first elements of H.R. 3000 to be reported from the subcommittee.

In May, 1963, it became evident that the House Education and Labor Committee would take up separately each element in the president's omnibus education bill when each was favorably reported from the subcommittee. Reports were expected next on vocational education and aid to federally impacted areas programs. Since these proposals related to popular, already existing programs, they were believed to have the best chance for inclusion in the new bill.

The ALA Washington Office advised the library community to temper their enthusiasm for their success. The fact that a number of controversial issues had been raised in the hearings and the failure of the full committee to report out the bill suggested that there was a vigorous debate going on within that committee. As the first segment of the education package to come up, H.R. 4879 would be drawing much of the fire directed at the administration's program and not at the public library proposals as such. At the hearings, congressmen on the committee repeatedly asked why the Library Services Act should be extended to urban areas when unfilled needs remained in rural communities. M. Gene Snyder (R-Kentucky) introduced excerpts from the U.S. Civil Rights Commission's 1961 report applying to the Library Services Act. The Civil Rights Commission had recommended that the Commissioner of Education determine whether or not public librarians receiving federal funds under LSA were practicing discrimination. In addition to this racial issue, the normal tendency of budget cutting continued to be raised.

Anthony J. Celebrezze, Secretary of HEW, appeared on April 29 as the first witness before the Senate Subcommittee on Education, chaired by Senator Wayne Morse (D-Oregon). Senator Winston Prouty (R-Vermont) asked if the administration had withheld aid to segregated rural public libraries, school districts, hospitals, agricultural colleges, and vocational training programs. The secretaary was asked further if he would object to a provision in the education bill forbidding funds to states where racial discrimination existed. Celebreeze replied that the education bill was "not intended to solve all the sins of the world." He expressed the belief that such a provision should be left to a civil rights bill and that if it were included in the education bill, "we will get no bill". (*ALA Washington Newsletter*, April 30, 1963, p. 3).

Support for the library legislation was expressed at the Senate hearings by Jennings Randolph (D-West Virginia) and Ralph Yarborough (D-Texas). Jacob Javits (R-New York), left the Senate floor where debate was being held on a hotly contested feed-grain bill to attend the hearings and speak briefly in behalf of the library program. Javits spoke of the "essentiality" of libraries to the nation's system of education. Libraries, he said, were as necessary as any part of the educational process and encouragement of library training should be on the same basis as teaching. At the Senate hearings there were a number of questions on the national need for school librarians.

On May 23, 1963, the House Committee on Education and Labor approved in a 22 to 5 vote the public library services and construction provisions in H.R. 4879. However, added to it was an amendment which cut off funds to segregated public libraries. Historically antisegregation amendments, often bearing the name "Powell Amendments" for Congressman Adam Clayton Powell, Chairman of the Committee, had been attached to bills as a device to kill a proposal without actually having to vote against it. There was little possibility of a bill so amended gaining approval of the House Rules Committee and reaching the floor for a vote.

Throughout the summer congressmen were concerned about the effectiveness of adding antidiscrimination amendments to bills before the House Education and Labor Committee. Thomas P. Gill (D-Hawaii) and 52 cosponsors had introduced a civil rights bill that was the focus of the debate. It would require that federal funds be withheld from existing programs, including the Library Services Act, where discrimination was practiced. On June 26, the House Subcommittee on Education held hearings on the Gill amendment. James Quigley, Assistant Secretary of

Health, Education, and Welfare, expressed his sympathies for the objectives of the bill but stated that the department preferred section 601 of the administration's new civil rights bill (H.R. 7152 and S. 1731). The chief distinctions made by Mr. Quigley were: (1) the Gill amendment would apply only to a few programs administered by the department whereas section 601 would apply to all programs. (2) the bill amendment makes mandatory the withholding of federal funds whereas section 601 permits the department discretion to withhold funds or not as it judges the national interest to be best served.

On June 27, 1963, L. Quincy Mumford, Librarian of Congress, testified before the Senate Subcommittee on Education in support of all the library aspects of the Senate version of the National Education Improvement Act of 1962.

On July 25, the House Committee on Education and Labor approved H.R. 4879, the Library Services and Construction Act, and sent it to the House Rules Committee. The "Powell Amendment" had been removed and a technical amendment had been added to include the District of Columbia under coverage of the new act. On August 5, the House Education and Labor Committee issued the printed report (H. Report 635) on H.R. 4879. All eighteen Democrats on the committee supported passage of the bill. Eight of the twelve Republican members of the committee signed in opposition to the report. The remaining four Republicans did not sign. The opposition gave four key reasons for opposing the bill: (1) The existing Library Services Act did not expire until June 30, 1966 and was designed to meet the most urgent needs. (2) Removal of the 10,000 population limitation is not needed and might harm the library service in rural areas. (3) In 1955, proponents of the legislation stated that the federal program for libraries would be terminal. (4) States and communities have not been willing to meet their responsibilities for public libraries.

In the Senate, however, by a unanimous vote of members present, the Senate Subcommittee on Education, chaired by Wayne Morse, approved for full committee consideration all four titles of the administration's National Education Improvement Act. The four titles included aid to schools in federally impacted areas, vocational education, the National Defense Education Act, and the Library Services and Construction Act. The library title was identical to that reported in the House. The Senate Subcommittee on Education used the Vocational Education Act of 1963 which had passed the House on August 6, 1963, as the vehicle to bring out the other three titles. On September 25, the full Senate Committee on Labor and Public Welfare reported favorably on the Library Services and Construction Act as one of four separate educational bills which would now go to the Senate floor. One of the other bills brought out at the same time was a higher education facilities bill, H.R. 6143, which included provisions for federal grants limited to the construction of science and engineering buildings and libraries.

On October 29, 1963, Senator Morse introduced the long-awaited Senate version of LSCA. S. 2265 was identical to H.R. 4879 except for some minor technical changes, including a change in the language of section 4 to emphasize the needs of people of all ages, including students, rather than "Students of all ages" as in the House bill.

This slight change in the language of the Senate bill, while not critical, was an example of the importance of clearing up ambiguity in the intent of a law. Doubtless this was Krettek's doing. Charlie Lee, who served on the Senate staff under Senator Wayne Morse, noted that Krettek was always welcome in their committee office because they could count on her word. Also, they knew if they were overlooking something in their committee report, she would bring it to their attention before they were irrevocably committed to the wrong language. Krettek was often allowed to see committee reports in preliminary form and to examine the language of a report.

Krettek on one occasion saw a preliminary report with language she just could not accept. One committee staffer would not agree with her recommended changes, so she had to go to the general counsel for the full committee, in this case, Jack Forsythe, of the Senate Labor and Public Welfare Committee. Forsythe agreed with Krettek's contention that the language was not acceptable and, said, "No, this language will not do." Krettek remembered that Forsythe took the biggest pair of scissors she ever saw from a desk drawer, cut the offending section out of the draft report and then asked her, "Now, what do you want?" The two of them then proceeded to draft language to go into the final report.

TRAGEDY AND TRIUMPH, NOVEMBER, 1963

Shortly after 1:00 P.M. on Friday, November 22, 1963, Senator Wayne Morse, sponsor and floor manager, introduced the Library Services and Construction Act on the floor of the Senate. Krettek, Lorenz, and Lee were present in the Senate chamber to follow the debate. Senator Edward Kennedy, the Democratic Senator from Massachusetts and brother of President John Kennedy, was presiding on the rostrum in the Vice-President's chair. A number of senators from both sides of the aisle had risen and spoken favorably for the bill. Senator Winston Prouty (R-Vermont), the ranking minority member of the Senate Labor and Public Welfare Committee, was at the microphone making a speech supporting the bill. In the midst of his speech there was an unusual clustering of Senators around the Clerk's desk.

Senator Morse interrupted, "Mr. President, (referring to the Chair, Senator Edward Kennedy) will the Senator from Vermont yield for an emergency?"
Mr. Prouty: "I yield."
Mr. Morse: "Mr. President, I suggest the absence of a quorum."
The Presiding Officer (Senator Kennedy): "The clerk will call the roll."

Senator Kennedy came down from the chair and rushed to the room behind the rostrum where the Associated Press teletype machines were located. The legislative clerk proceeded to call the roll.

Mr. Morse: "Mr. President, I ask unanimous consent that the order for the quorum call be withdrawn."
The Presiding Officer (Mr. Holland in the chair): "Without objection, it is so ordered."
Mr. Mansfield: "Mr. President, I ask unanimous consent that on the pending measure there be a time allocated of 1 hour on each amendment and 1 hour on the bill."
The Presiding Officer: "Is there objection to the unanimous-consent request? Does the majority leader desire to have included the regular provisions as to germaneness?"
Mr. Mansfield: "The regular provisions."
Mr. Morse: "Mr. President, I should like to interrupt a moment to say that if ever there was an hour when all Americans should pray, this is the hour" (*Congressional Record*, Volume 109, part 17, p. 22692).

Eventually the exact horror of this emergency became known to Krettek and Lorenz sitting in the gallery. President John F. Kennedy had been assassinated. However, when the Senate adjourned the death of the president had not yet been confirmed.

Krettek vividly remembers that afternoon. She went out into the hall and saw one of Senator Hubert Humphrey's administrative assistants sitting there and cried on his shoulder. She had been scheduled to fly to Chicago that afternoon to report to the ALA Executive Board on the bill. It was expected that it would pass easily.

Charlie Lee recalled that all parts of the Library Services and Construction Act did not have clear sailing up to the time the floor debate was interrupted.

The construction part of the act was in serious and grave danger when it was on the floor of the Senate. It had announced opposition from some fairly conservative members from the mountain states. The member who was particularly exercised, even though his State Librarian who also happened to be the Republican Committeewoman from that state, had spoken in favor of the program. Nevertheless, he felt that this was not an area where the federal government should be putting money.

... Even Senator Javits was worried about bricks and mortar. His view, which was expressed one time in a mark-up session was that generally you can get someone to put up money for a building because they got their name on it. This was in terms of the college libraries and the college construction. But it was important to get the services out and therefore with limited resources that is where the money should go.

So, we really didn't know whether or not we would be able to get construction through the Senate. Then, of course, that was resolved tragically by the dramatic scene on the floor [when Kennedy was assassinated]. . . . The Senate . . . suspended immediately after a prayer. And when we came back into session after the funeral, the act was picked up and [at] that point the sentiment of the Senate had crystallized and the sentiment of the House had crystallized. This bill passed really as a memorial tribute to President Kennedy. It's a macabre association but it did save the construction authority. In a sense, every library in the country that was built or renovated since that time has been a partial Presidential library by implication.

Indeed, on Tuesday, November 26, 1963, when the Senate resumed, the Library Services and Construction Act was the first bill brought up. In less than one hour several technical amendments and one major amendment were proposed and approved. The principal amendment, introduced by Senator Gordon Allott (R-Colorado), accepted by Senator Morse, and approved by voice vote, established a ceiling of $25 million for services and $20 million for construction for each of the three years under which the act was effective. This eliminated a so-called open-end authorization section in the original bill which called for $20 million for construction in fiscal 1964 and such sums as Congress may determine for the next two years. Senator Allott had originally introduced a proposal to have eliminated altogether the authorization of funds for buildings but he later withdrew it.

The final vote on passage of LSCA in the Senate was 89 to 7. On Friday, December 13, 1963, the House Rules Committee granted an open rule for one hour of debate on H.R. 4879, the Library Services Act. The House floor vote was set for the week of January 21, 1964, in the Second Session of the Eighty-seventh Congress.

The passage of the Library Services and Construction Act in the House took four hours. Supporters had to fend off a number of crippling amendments. The most drastic of these were the amendments by Peter Frelinghuysen (R-New Jersey) to set a new population limit of 20,000 instead of complete elimination of the then current population limitation; a change of the authorization for services to $15 million; and the complete elimination of the construction title. Congressman Freylinghuysen's amendments lost by the narrow margin of 179 in favor to 183 opposed.

The final vote on passage of the bill in the House was 254 in favor to 107 opposed.

Because of the differences between the House and Senate versions of the act, the Senate on January 30, 1964, voted to concur in the amendments of the House to the Senate Bill 2265. The act moved speedily to the White House where President Lyndon B. Johnson signed it into law on February 11, 1964.

Chapter 7

Lyndon Johnson and the Great Society (1963-68)

Upon the death of President Kennedy on November 22, 1963 Vice-President Lyndon Baines Johnson assumed the presidency. Johnson carried forward the slain president's program with all the resources at his disposal—and those resources were formidable. He may very well have been the most politically astute president in our history. Certainly the massive domestic programs launched during his administrations equalled or even surpassed Franklin Roosevelt's New Deal. He called his dream the "Great Society." The emphases on welfare, civil rights, and education were designed to fulfill the promises of the American dream. And he invoked the rhetoric of the slain president in an early effort to pass his programs. Johnson's first State of the Union Message to a joint session of Congress on Wednesday, January 8, 1964, gave a prominence to libraries that they never had before. It was the first, and only time, that libraries have been included in a president's State of the Union Message.

In his introductory statements, the president said,

> Last year's congressional session was the longest in peace time history. With that foundation, let us work together to make this year's session the best in the Nation's history.
>
> Let this session of Congress be known as the session which did more for civil rights than the last hundred sessions combined; as the session which enacted the most far-reaching tax cut of our time; as the session which declared all-out war on human poverty and unemployment in these United States; as the session which finally recognized the health needs of all our older citizens; as the session which reformed our tangled transportation and transit policies; as the session which achieved the most effective, efficient foreign aid program ever; and as the session which

69

helped to build more homes, more schools, MORE LIBRARIES, [emphasis added] and more hospitals than any single session of Congress in the history of our Republic.

... This administration today, here and now, declares unconditional war on poverty in America.

... We must build more libraries in every area and more hospitals and nursing homes under the Hill-Burton Act, and train more nurses.

... These programs are obviously not for the poor or the underprivileged alone. Every American will benefit by the extension of social security to cover the hospital costs of their aged parents. Every American community will benefit from the construction or modernization of schools, LIBRARIES, hospitals and nursing homes and from the improvement of urban renewal in public transit.

... My good friends and fellow Americans: In these last seven sorrowful weeks, we have learned anew that nothing is so enduring as faith, and nothing is so degrading as hate.

John Kennedy was a victim of hate, but he was also a great builder of faith—faith in our fellow Americans, whatever their creed or their color or their stations in life; faith in the future of man, whatever his divisions and differences. ... So I ask you now in the Congress and in the country to join with me in expressing and fulfilling that faith in working for a nation, a nation that is free from want and a world that is free from hate—a world of peace and justice, and freedom and abundance, for our time and for all time to come.

There was no doubt about the enthusiastic reception to Johnson's speech. It was interrupted by applause more than eighty times. He had captured the pent-up emotions of a country wracked by grief and ready to respond to the New Frontier vision of his predecessor.

The mention of libraries in the State of the Union message was no accident. When the ALA Committee on Legislation had talked with Theodore Sorenson and Mike Feldman, they asked that libraries be included in the next presidential address. However, after the assassination, ALA officials had not been in contact with the White House and everything just drifted. Bessie Moore recalled that when she heard the president's message she knew that Sorenson had not forgotten his promises. Also, it was obvious, she stated, "By that time Johnson had bought the program thoroughly and probably did better with it than Kennedy would have done. ... Johnson, as far as I can tell, did everything he could to carry out Kennedy's wishes. I think it is generally accepted that he really tried."

FINAL PASSAGE OF THE LIBRARY SERVICES AND CONSTRUCTION ACT IN CONGRESS

On January 21, 1964, the House passed the Library Services and Construction Act by a 254 to 107 roll call vote, and returned it to the Senate with amendments. The margin of the final vote is deceptive. There was a very tough battle on the floor to fight off amendments offered by Republicans to kill both the construction and urban aid aspects of the bill.

As previously noted, supporters of the bill had narrowly defeated the Frelinghuysen amendment to raise the population limit only to 20,000, thus excluding urban areas, and removing the construction title of the bill. A vote to recommit the bill in order to delete the construction sections, offered by David T. Martin (R-Nebraska) was defeated on a 174 to 188 roll call vote. The opponents of the bill said that it contradicted the intent of the 1956 Library Services Act and that the bill's construction provisions in effect constituted a new federal program. Also, Republican members of the House Education and Labor Committee were incensed when Adam Clayton Powell (D-New York), Chairman of the committee, without clearing the action with them, began to offer amendments to make the bill conform to the Senate version and thus avoid a conference.

The Frelinghuysen amendment, initially accepted on a 138 to 121 teller vote, while eliminating construction and urban aid, would have doubled the existing authorization from $7.5 million to $15 million annually. An amendment which would have ensured that rural areas would be allotted as much as they received in fiscal 1963 for library services was rejected by a voice vote. Congressman John H. Dent (D-Pennsylvania), Chairman of the Select Subcommittee on Education and floor manager of the bill, assured the House that the bill already contained adequate safeguards against depletion of funds for rural districts.

> The Public library is in a strategic position to play an important role in the fight on poverty and its cause; it can aid adults and those who are engaged directly in assisting the impoverished youths to gain education and training . . . in short, the public library is now widely recognized as a vital cultural and economic resource as well as a fundamental educational institution. . . . Serious deficiencies in public libraries exist throughout the Nation. For example, 18 million persons are without public libraries and 110 million are hampered by trying to use seriously inadequate facilities (*Congressional Record*, 88th Congress 2nd Sess. (1964), CX, Pt. 1, p. 770).

Two amendments by Albert H. Quie (R-Minnesota) were accepted on voice votes. One delayed implementation of the urban library aid provisions of the bill until fiscal 1965. The other reinserted language from the 1956 Act to require that state plans concentrate on areas without library services or with inadequate services.

The Senate on January 30, 1964, agreed by voice vote to the House amendments to the Library Services and Construction Act, clearing the bill for the president's signature. In final form the Act contained the following key provisions:

1. The present population limitation was removed beginning July 1, 1964, thus extending benefits to all areas of the country regardless of size.

2. The previous basic allotment (a) to Guam, American Samoa, and the Virgin Islands was increased from $10,000 to $25,000 and (b) to each of the states from $40,000 to $100,000. The base year was changed from fiscal 1956 to fiscal 1963.

3. The new construction title was added, for which $20 million was authorized in fiscal 1964.

4. The District of Columbia was brought into the coverage of the Act. (This made the Washington, D.C. Public Library the only combination state and public library in the country.)

5. For fiscal years 1965 and 1966 funds for services and construction were authorized for "such sums as Congress may determine."

Throughout the Spring of 1964, library supporters continued their fight to gain larger appropriations for the Library Services and Construction Act. They were greatly encouraged by President Johnson's sensitivity to their cause. On February 4, 1964, after three decades of effort, the library community and their allies gathered at the White House for the first presidential signing ceremony for a federal library bill.

THE BILL SIGNING CEREMONY

According to Krettek the guests went over to the White House for the signing ceremony in the midst of a heavy snowstorm. Leaders in Congress, including Congressman Fogarty, Senator Hill, Senator Morse, Senator Aiken, Congressmen Mills and Elliott, and officials from HEW and USOE attended. Library leaders from throughout the country were there including all the members of the ALA Committee on Legislation: Emerson Greenaway, Ed Low, Bessie Moore, Cora Paul Bomar, Lucille Nix, and Richard Sealock. Not overlooked were the ALA staff: David Clift, ALA Executive Director, and Germaine Krettek.

Bessie Moore had received her invitation to attend the signing ceremony via a telephone call while she was visiting a small rural school in Alma, Arkansas. The secretary in the little school raced down the hall and said, "Oh, come quick Mrs. Moore, the White House is calling."

All ALA committee members received pens used by the president in signing the bill. Krettek recalled that Fred Wagman, the ALA President, had brought in, concealed under his coat, a large, 24" x 16" framed picture of the National Library Week Proclamation. At the conclusion of the ceremony, he whipped it out and handed it to President Johnson. With the memory of the assassination of President Kennedy still in her mind, she wondered how Wagman had managed to get that kind of package past the security guards.

APPROPRIATIONS FOR LSCA AND FEDERAL LIBRARY LEGISLATION FOR 1964 AND 1965

Gaining the initial appropriations for the Library Services and Construction Act proved a long and arduous process. On February 26, 1964, at a meeting of the Senate Subcommittee on Appropriations for the Health, Education, and Welfare Department, USOE Commissioner Francis Keppel requested $55 million for LSCA for 1965. There was then a delay. From April through May, action in the Senate was held up by a filibuster conducted by southern Senators opposed to the passage of the 1964 Civil Rights Act. On June 10, 1964, Senator Everett Dirksen (R-Illinois), speaking in behalf of a compromise bill, had mustered the necessary two-thirds vote needed to invoke cloture, thus ending the debate and allowing the Civil Rights bill, which had already passed the House, to come to a vote on June 17, 1964.

In the House, no appropriations for LSCA had been included in the 1965 appropriations bill because the Bureau of the Budget had not transmitted the president's request for funds until five days after the House Appropriations Subcommittee had closed its hearings. Therefore the House bill included no appropriations for LSCA. The 1965 House Appropriations bill, minus funds for libraries, passed overwhelmingly 344 to 20 on April 14, 1964, and was sent to the Senate. Chairman Fogarty commented, "As far as I am concerned, if the budget had been in the bill before us we would have the $55 million for library services."

However, on August 19, 1964, the Senate approved the HEW appropriations bill, including $55 million for LSCA. On September 3, 1964, both House and Senate agreed on this amount for 1965. In the ensuing delay, and because of Quie's amendment, one year's authorization for LSCA, fiscal year 1964 had been lost.

In a related action on October 3, 1964, Congress approved amendments extending the National Defense Education Act for three more years at a level of $348,603,000 for 1965. Most important to the library community, in addition to funds for equipment, audio-visual materials, and print materials, Title XI called for institutes for reading, teachers of disadvantaged youth, school library personnel, educational media specialists, and supervisors of such personnel.

October 16, 1964, representatives of the American Library Association ended their legislative year as they had begun it—in the White House. There in the East Room they attended the signing of the NDEA Extension by President Johnson.

By April 11, 1965, the president had gained the passage of his Elementary and Secondary Education Act which provided under Title II for $100 million in support of school libraries. By October, 1965, the Higher Education Act had passed and authorized $70 million for academic libraries but did not fund them. In 1965, funds for medical libraries were provided with the passage of the Medical Library Assistance Act on October 1, 1965.

EXTENSION OF THE LIBRARY SERVICES ACT—1966

Congressman Carl Perkins introduced H.R. 12133, a bill to extend the Library Services and Construction Act, on January 18, 1966. Included was a new Title III to stimulate interlibrary cooperation. Senator George McGovern (D-South Dakota) introduced a companion bill in the Senate two days later. The extension of LSCA gained bi-partisan support when a third bill was introduced on February 18, by Senators Jacob Javits (R-New York), John Sherman Cooper (R-Kentucky), and Winston Prouty (R-Vermont). Their bill added another concept to LSCA, Title IV-Specialized State Library Services. This provision authorized grants to state library agencies for five years to strengthen library services to persons in state-operated institutions, such as prison inmates, hospital patients, the aged, handicapped, mentally ill, and orphans.

Introduction of extension legislation was matched by the inclusion of authorizations for LSCA in the president's budget request to Congress. In his Domestic Health and Education Message (House Document 395) on March 1, 1966, President Johnson recommended the LSCA extension. He recommended an authorization for Title I for fiscal year 1967 of $27.5 million, up $2.5 million from 1966, and such sums as may be necessary for each of the following four succeeding years. He asked for $30 million for Title II-Library Construction, which was the same as for 1966, and such sums as may be necessary for each of the four succeeding years. In his remarks to Congress, President Johnson stated,

Those who do not read are not much better off than those who cannot read. More than 100 million Americans have inadequate public library services. More than 15 million none at all.

A Library must be a living institution with trained staff and funds to obtain new books, periodicals, films, records, and other material.

As the boundaries of learning are pushed back, our need for storehouse of knowledge grows greater. They offer man his link with the past and his vision of the future.

Most public libraries in the United States are poorly equipped to perform this vital role (ALA *Washington Newsletter*, March 11, 1966, p. 1-2).

By March 14, 1966, Senator Lister Hill had 52 cosponsors (a majority of the Senate) for extension of LSCA. Bi-partisan support for the bill was strong and forty states were represented among the bill's sponsors.

On March 29, 1966, Congressman Roman Pucinski (D-Illinois) introduced another bill for the LSCA extension. As Chairman of the Select Education Subcommittee of the House Committee on Education and Labor, he called for a hearing on his bill and similar bills for April 19, 20, and 21. By April 27, 1966, Congressman Pucinski could report that the full committee had approved H.R. 14050, his version of the LSCA extension bill. In the report of the committee, Pucinski stated that only two of the thirty-one members of the full committee did not accept the majority opinion and then only on the basis of the amounts appropriated.

Time and time again in the hearings the proponents stressed the importance of cooperation and coordination of library services. Their major point of difference was in the amount of funds to be authorized. Administration witnesses, including HEW Secretary John Gardner and U.S. Commissioner of Education, Harold Howe, II, endorsed the objectives and needs for the legislation, but urged the limitation of funds to those proposed in the administration bill, $57.5 million, because of current budgetary restrictions and other domestic and international commitments. However, the committee chose to authorize $73 million for all four titles of LSCA (Title I—$35 million, Title II—$40 million, Title III—$5 million, and Title IV—$8 million). Further, they recommended $10 million increases for the other titles for 1968 through 1971.

Unlike previous years when the extension of the Library Services Act was considered, the House Rules Committee granted a rule in less than a week for May 25, 1966 to allow two hours of debate on the LSCA extension bill. During the previous week, on May 20, 1966, the Senate Labor and Public Welfare Committee, chaired by Senator Lister Hill, had held hearings on the Senate version of the bill, S. 3076.

In a notable departure from the 1964 session, the House in less than the two-hour debate time allotted, at 2:50 P.M. June 2, 1966, passed the Library Services and Construction Act Amendments of 1966 (H.R. 14050) by a sweeping bi-partisan vote of 336 to 2. Ninety-two congressmen did not vote, but many of the absences occurred because of last minute changes in the schedule for the debate. Congressman Pucinski, who managed the bill on the floor, stressed the amazing response of local communities to the legislation and extolled LSCA as a model of federal grant legislation for preserving local and state responsibility and stimulating increased financial support for libraries. In less than five minutes time, at 3:00 P.M. on June 22, 1966, the Senate passed its version of the House bill, with the same authorizations but with several other technical differences. On June 28, the House, by unanimous consent, agreed to concur with the Senate passed version of the Library Services and Construction Act Amendments of 1966.

THE NATIONAL ADVISORY COMMISSION ON LIBRARIES

On July 19, 1966, President Johnson signed the 1966 LSCA Amendments into law. In signing the bill, the president announced that he would name a National Commission on Libraries. This idea had first emerged during the previous administration. After describing current expenditures for federal library programs, he argued for a commission:

> But money alone will not do the job. We need intelligent advice and planning to see that our millions are spent wisely and well. We need to take a close look at the future of our libraries. We need to ask some serious questions.
> What part can libraries play in the Nation's rapidly developing communications and information-exchange networks? Computers and new information technology have brought us to the brink of dramatic changes in library technique. As we face this information revolution, we want to be satisfied that our funds do not preserve library practices which are already obsolete.
> Are our federal efforts to assist libraries intelligently administered—or are they too fragmented among separate programs and agencies.
> To deal with these and other questions, I will soon name a National Library Commission of distinguished citizens and experts. Its job will be to point toward an effective and efficient library system for the future. The Commission will report directly to the Secretary of Health, Education, and Welfare. It can provide a national perspective on the problems that confront our Nation's libraries. (*ALA Washington Newsletter*, July 21, 1966, pp. 1-2).

On September 2, 1966, President Johnson, in Executive Order 11301, established the President's Committee on Libraries under the chairmanship of John W. Gardner, the Secretary of Health, Education, and Welfare. To assist the committee in appraising the role of libraries, President Johnson appointed a National Advisory Commission on Libraries, composed of distinguished citizens and experts to be headed by Douglas Knight, President of Duke University. Among the distinguished citizens serving on the commission were former Congressman Carl Elliott, Emerson Greenaway, and Bessie Moore.

Elliott remembered being involved in planning the hearings held by the commission in 1967. His former administrative assistant, Mary Allen Jolley, who had scheduled his hearings around the country when he was a congressman, was responsible for making the arrangements for the commission meetings. He recalls that, "[We] tried to spot the hearings in such places as would illustrate the library needs of that and similar areas, but also that would spotlight so far as the representative of that area of Congress was concerned. What we were trying to do was kill as many birds with one stone as we could." Consequently, it was no accident that hearings were held in Pikeville, Kentucky, the home district of Congressman Carl Perkins of the Committee on Education and Labor, and Lubbock, Texas, the home of Congressman George Mahon, Chairman of the House Appropriations Committee.

The hearing in Pikeville, Kentucky, on October 20, 1967, was one of the memorable occasions in library history. Participants were enthusiastic and the Advisory Commission members were impressed. According to Elliott, "I think it was one of the best library hearings of any kind that I ever attended over a long period of interest in libraries." On the videotapes Ed Holley's invitation to the panel to "Tell me about Pikeville" resulted in a dialogue between Elliott and Moore which seems worth reporting here in detail.

Carl Elliott:

Pikeville is little town of five thousand, situated there in the mountains of eastern Kentucky. It's in Congressman Carl Perkins' district and we decided that that might be a good place to hold the hearings. We would get at least the mountain viewpoint from that vantage.

I think it was one of the best library hearings of any kind or nature that I have ever attended over a long period of interest in libraries. We had people who had literally come out of the mountains there to make themselves and their attitudes and their knowledge known. We had ladies with bonnets and high topped shoes, who came to express themselves. Bessie and I were talking last night about the rural mail carrier, who came to say what he felt about it. And we had the wonderful mayor of that town of Pikeville, who had an unusually large and expansive fund of information and imagination and brains and everything else. He not only came to our hearings but he came down and sat with us on the nights that we were there. Two or three days, he would come and spend the night with us talking about, you know, the general overall outlook.

. . . That was an outpouring of democratic interest in libraries and library information the like of which I haven't seen anything greater in my time.

I think back of the hearings all across the country. For example, we went into the area of Pennsylvania that was down and out on the account that at that time the coal mines were not in recession but in depression. I got some ideas there in Pennsylvania that had never occurred to me before. The same was true all over the country. I thought that those hearings (and will for the future and for some time in the future) constitute a base of information the like of which there is not in America.

. . . And I want to say that Emerson Greenaway was further from the center of those operations than anyone could be just about. But he took great pride in attending the meetings, every one he could, and for furnishing, as Emerson always does, something for people to think about. Something for me to think about. Emerson always leaves a thought. And it's a good thought. And whoever originated, 'Keep a good thought,' when I hear that I think of Emerson Greenaway. He always gives good thoughts for libraries.

Not too much came, if you want to look at it that a way, of those hearings. Although we did create the National Commission that Bessie Moore is the Vice-Chairman of. We made at least that much progress as a result, Bessie. And you all have been able to study and make recommendations and observations and conclusions about the library program of America and it's been very, very helpful. This is a thing, as we have pointed out, that doesn't move very fast.

Ed Holley:

It's probably unfortunate that that report came out right at the end of an administration. That was one of the unfortunate things politically. Bessie, you tell us about those hearings and about what the postmaster said and about South Dakota.

Bessie Moore:

Well, I disagree with Carl on one point. I think the hearings did have great effect. When we are talking about amassing public opinion and having people be conscious of the needs of libraries, I think the hearings did a great deal. And of course, the very first recommendation, [was for a permanent commission] we had five recommendations of the commission, and incidentally, I would like to brag a little. I am the only person still sitting on the commission that was on the first commission. I am the only survivor.

. . . But anyway, those hearings were effective in that regard. They awakened people all over because the librarians and the trustees saw to it that all points of view, almost, were represented in those hearings. They got the people out. And the press was great. The state presses, and the regional presses. Good news coverage and publicity. And I think good professional publicity. Some were poor but most were good. It depends upon the editor, you know. I don't ever worry about the bad things in the press. The old joke is, 'just spell my name right.' They talked about libraries and that was the main thing.

Of course, their first recommendation was that we have a permanent commission. And that was accomplished. And hopefully we will be in business for a long time to come. This is not the time or the place to talk about the accomplishments of the commission. But I think the commission is necessary for the progress of libraries in this country and for the relationships between the administrations. This is because the commission reports both to the president and to Congress. It is an independent commission and that is very important and necessary to its proper function.

About the Pikeville meeting, I remember the mail carrier who said that he really thought that the federal government ought to supply free postage for people getting materials from libraries. He made a good justification for it. I don't know how he would have been listened to in Congress, Carl, but he certainly made a good case of how little it would cost and what the cost benefit would be. Then, to get back to the Bismarck hearing. This was Bismarck, North Dakota. There are four of us, I believe, who went out to that hearing. You didn't go [to] that one, Emerson. Dr. Hubbard, who was Dean of the College of Medicine of the University of Michigan, Carl and I, and I can't remember who the fourth person was. I believe it was the President of the Carnegie Commission.

Carl Elliott:
Mr. Haskins.

Bessie Moore:
Well, finally everybody had made plane reservations for a time when they thought we would be through. And they finally left. Because I was chairman of the hearings, I had decided to stay all night. I didn't know what might come up. When ten-thirty came, we still had witnesses that hadn't been heard. So I said if anybody wants to testify, I will stay until they are heard. And I stayed until midnight. The people in North Dakota had driven hundreds of miles and they wanted to be heard. Now I don't think . . . those kind of hearings—the effect lasts a long time—(*Holley*: 'Democracy in action.') And so when the commission was organized, when the National Commission was set up, the first thing we did was to organize hearings again over the country. Because those had been so successful.

Of course, we took them to different parts of the country and had a different focus. But I think they were equally helpful.

Ed Holley:
It's really an important thing to do in a country as large as this is. Not just population-wise but geographically, to get government as close to people as possible. I think you were talking, Gerrie, about the necessity of building public support. We sometimes forget what an enormous country this is. You only have to try to go from the East Coast as we do in North Carolina, all the way to the West to realize that we are really covering a lot of territory.

Bessie Moore:
And a lot of different mores and a lot of different . . .

Ed Holley:
And what works in Iowa doesn't necessarily work in North Carolina, and so forth. But it does strike me that one of the things that you did in the original Act and kept in all the subsequent acts, and Carl I think you can speak to this as one of the obstacles that had to be overcome, was the fact that so much emphasis was placed on determination of services, collections, book collections, whatever, would be determined in the state and the locality.

Carl Elliott:
. . . we were trying to convince everybody that there is no impingement on states' rights, that there is no racial question in this bill. That's the reason that we wrote all the states' rights provisions in the bill. I thought then and I think now that that was one of the bill's strengths. It encouraged the states themselves to get out and start a state program of aid to libraries.

. . . Library Services Act . . . did a tremendous good for the development of a sense of importance, the political importance of libraries in the southern states.

As Bessie Moore indicated, the findings and recommendations of the National Advisory Commission on Libraries did result in legislation to create a permanent National Commission on Libraries and Information cience (NCLIS). This NCLIS bill was passed by the Senate on May 23, 1969 and by the House on April 20, 1970. Signed by President Richard Nixon on July 20, 1970, Public Law 91-345 has achieved a number of the objectives originally envisioned by its supporters. Equally important from the National Advisory Commission was the publication of *Libraries at Large*, a record of the Advisory Commission's activities and a permanent reminder that the commission achieved President Johnson's goal of "intelligent advice and planning" for the future of libraries in America.

IMPACT OF LSCA AND THE OTHER LIBRARY LEGISLATION OF THE SIXTIES

That federal library legislation, and the appropriations to support it, expanded significantly in the sixties no one can deny. Users of all types of libraries were the beneficiaries. With the tremendous resources of the federal government stimulating the states and localities, there were new library buildings for colleges, universities, and public libraries; new book and nonprint materials for all types of libraries; and school and public libraries in places where they had never existed before. The post-World War II baby boom created the need and a sympathetic administration and Congress took steps to meet that need.

Regarding the impact of the Library Services and Construction Act in the 1960s Emerson Greenaway stated,

> I think that one of the great advantages of the passage of the Library Services Act (and the Library Services and Construction) was the fact that it presented a great challenge to librarians to come up with some thoughtful innovations and improvements in library services.
> . . . [The increased funding for LSCA for services and construction and the stimulation of larger local appropriations] . . . The whole bill snowballed the fiscal arrangements of libraries.
> One of the outgrowths of this increased ability to work out problems came about where we found out that not only did we need the multi-county library system but we needed to go across state boundaries. Interstate compacts came about as one result of this.

And the Act did achieve its goal of stimulating the states and localities. Roger McDonough recalled that in New Jersey

> very few library buildings had been erected since the Carnegie days early in the century, a very few in the WPA days, but in the ten years that our state library was in charge of dispensing federal funds under very strict rules and so on, we helped build or remodel seventy-five public libraries in New Jersey. . . . The dramatic effects of this building resulted in overnight doubling of circulation.

In responding to the statement that for every dollar the federal government put into the LSCA for construction there were three, or four dollars of local and state money added to that, McDonough commented, "In our state it was eight times [that] at least. They would put up a building, an $800,000 building, and we would give them $50,000 as a grant. Rarely did we give $100,000, and then only for a regional library."

Another impact of the passage of LSCA in 1964, and ESEA and HEA in 1965, was the recognition these new programs brought increased responsibility for officials in the library unit within the U.S. Office of Education. That responsibility was reflected in greater status within USOE when, in 1964, the Library Services Branch became the Library Services Division. In 1964, Lorenz reported to the ALA Committee on Legislation that there were 43 staff members within the Library Services Branch and another 33 within the Adult Education Branch. From six staff members in 1956 the Division had grown by 1964 to include 80.

In 1965 the library unit was placed under the newly created Bureau of Adult and Vocational Education and was known as the Division of Library Services and Educational Facilities. Kathleen Molz describes these transformations of the library unit within the USOE in her book, *Federal Policy and Library Support*.

However, legislative successes and growth in appropriations for libraries and education and shifting responsibilities within the U.S. Office of Education had negative effects, as well. In our oral history discussions, the 1967 attempt at decentralization, or the establishing of regional offices, of the library unit and educational units provoked the most discussion. Regionalization was an attempt to grapple with all the problems inherent in administering a vastly expanded program of library and education aid.

The reorganization was imposed by the Department of Health, Education, and Welfare and did not come from a recommendation by the library community said Roger McDonough and John Lorenz. Elizabeth Hughey Arline, who experienced the reorganization from the perspective of a former state librarian and then as a staff member, felt,

> it was a mixed bag. It was very good to have a consultant close to the state agencies and who were directing the programs. . . . On the other hand, there was the feeling that we were not exactly quite sure what everyone else was doing. We didn't get a complete overall picture as quickly as we wanted. In fact, because of the different levels of operations among regions [there were nine regions], it was very difficult to get the facts and to maintain uniformity of administration because each of the OE Regions was a law unto itself.

"We in the field," said Roger McDonough, who was State Librarian of New Jersey, "felt that we were one more step from the fount."

Eileen Cooke, who was in contact with the various regions because the ALA Washington Office was a conduit between Washington and the field, said "the strong impression that I had was that the library program people out at the regional level didn't have the backup support staff that they needed. They were perceived to be closer to the people but they had six or eight states they were supposed to be close to and they might be assigned one-third of a secretary, shared with other regional specialists."

Another problem noted John Lorenz, who directed the division before it was regionalized,

> the staff was reduced. The regional offices, and the people responsible for the Library Services Act, could and in fact, were assigned to other programs either in addition to, or in place of, library services programs. . . . They were in the very difficult position of being responsible in two different directions, which should never happen administratively. They were responsible to the regional head and also responsible to Washington. It put them in a very difficult operating position.

The continuous reorganization of the Office of Education throughout the sixties and seventies was a fact of life for the staff. Often to make clear the priority Congress placed on certain USOE programs, laws were amended to force the designation of a specific unit with appropriate staff even though the appropriations for that part of the program might have been miniscule in terms of OE's total budget. The problem has not yet been resolved.

The growing cost of the war in Vietnam, the antiwar protest on college and university campuses, and President Johnson's decision not to seek re-election mark the end of the Great Society era. Although the benefits from the Johnson-initiated legislation would continue, the nation longed for a more tranquil period in which to consolidate some of society's gains as well as bring under control some of the successes.

More closely related to the Library Services and Contruction Act programs, the late sixties marked the end of the careers of two of the principal supporters of library legislation in Congress, Senator Lister Hill of Alabama and Congressman John Fogarty of Rhode Island.

Senator Hill announced his retirement in January, 1968, after forty-five years of service in Congress, fifteen in the House and thirty in the Senate. Lister Hill had begun his congressional career in 1923 at the age of twenty-nine. As the first Senate sponsor for the Rural Library Services Demonstration Bill in 1946, Senator Hill continued his support of libraries throughout his congressional career. During all of his thirty years in the Senate, he served as a member, and in 1955 assumed the chairmanship, of the Senate Committee on Labor and Public Welfare. At the same time, he served as the Chairman of the Senate Appropriations Subcommittee for the Departments of Labor and Health, Education, and Welfare. He was, thus, in the unique position of being in charge both of the committee authorizing the important social programs of his time and also being chairman of the Senate committee that approved the funds required to carry them out.

On June 21, 1956, immediately after the passage of the Library Services Act, the American Library Association awarded Senator Lister Hill an Honorary Life Membership,

> In recognition of distinguished service to libraries, especially as the original sponsor in 1946, and for continued leadership which resulted in the enactment, in 1956, of legislation whereby provision is now made for further extension and development of public library service in rural areas.

Again, upon the announcement of his retirement, the American Library Association recognized Senator Hill with a special Certificate of Commendation approved at the 87th ALA Annual Conference in Kansas City on June 28, 1968.

Eighteen months earlier John Fogarty had died suddenly of a heart attack on the morning of January 10, 1967, at the age of 54. He, too, had been a "long-time, powerful, and devoted friend of libraries" and was given ALA's highest award, Honorary Membership, in July, 1966. Fogarty first entered the U.S. House of Representatives in 1941, after winning his first political campaign in 1940 at the age of twenty-seven. Before going to Congress, he had been a bricklayer and had served as President of the Bricklayers and Masons Union, Local No. 1 of Rhode Island. In 1947, he was appointed to the House Appropriations Subcommittee for the Labor Department and Federal Security Agency, which in 1953 became the Department of Health, Education, and Welfare. In 1949, he became Chairman of the Subcommittee, a post he held except for 1953-54, when the Republicans controlled the House of Representatives, until his death.

James Stewart Healey's biography, *John E. Fogarty; Political Leadership for Library Development,* (1974) provides an excellent overview of his career as it relates to library legislation. Healey credits Fogarty's efforts in behalf of six library bills as being crucial for their successful passage during 1960-67: (1) The Extension of LSA, 1960; (2) The Interstate Compact, which he proposed in 1961; (3) The Omnibus Library Bill, 1961; (4) The Library Services and Construction Act, 1963; (5) The Medical Library Assistance Act of 1965; and (6) The LSCA Amendments, 1966.

Representative Fogarty's contributions to the library cause have been reflected throughout this report. The participants in this oral project remember him fondly. Gerrie Krettek worked closely with him while she was the ALA Washington Office Director and noted that he would frequently introduce her all over the country as "Our Miss Books."

Charlie Lee, who worked on the Senate Labor and Public Welfare Committee under Senator Hill, observed that,

> One of the things that allowed this progress [in library legislation] to be made is, I think, due in large part to the fact that Senator Hill and Mr. Fogarty on the House side, who had it within their prerogatives to kill the program with no appeal from that decision, and despite their own constituencies and where they came from, treated library programs as generously as they did anything but the major health programs. I think I have to add that little caveat because that [health programs] is where Lister's heart was.
>
> . . . Senator Hill also was one of the few major statesmen in the Senate, I think, over time. He had a long-range vision and he was extraordinarily patient. I remember one time when he passed a very minor health bill [at an] executive session of the committee, he pushed back his chair and said, 'Gentlemen, that completes twelve years of work on my part. Now all we have to do is to get it through the House.'

In observing how power was distributed in the Senate in the 1950s and the position of Senator Hill in the power structure, Lee states,

> The Chief Counsel explained to me how the system worked. . . . A newly elected Senator from the southern states was told which committee he would go to, and the same was true of the House. If they were good boys, after a certain amount of time, they were told they would become chairman and be able to do good things for their states and constituencies. But meantime since we [the southern Senators] are representing a part of the country that doesn't have much wealth, we had better be able to outthink them. The best way to outthink them was to have the votes on the committees that controlled the destinies. Finally, it came to the point where education became a part of the Senate Committee on Labor and Public Welfare. They [the southern Senators] had to give up some bastions, so they left Lister Hill there because they knew that everybody loved and respected him. They knew that he would protect their vital interests, and at the same time they put all the liberals on one committee so that they would do the least harm. And leave the really important agricultural committees to the South.
>
> It was because they [Hill and Fogarty] did exercise this kind of statesmanlike vision, recognizing that the country was changing, and that this was a movement whose time had come, and was overdue. Despite what one would call the political constraints, they had the courage to do what they did. I think that they deserve a lot of credit.

According to John Lorenz, John Fogarty was a

> bricklayer from Rhode Island who had that kind of vision and love for libraries and books. . . . He was a very important factor on the House side as a co-equal, you might say, in terms of appropriations with Lister Hill. [Charlie Lee interjected: "From the standpoint of the House, Fogarty was the superior man because the House originated the appropriations.] . . . And of course, the communication between the two was superb in terms of what one could not take care of on the one side the other could take care of on the other side.

In commenting on Fogarty's love for libraries, Roger McDonough observes, "And it was for real. And, we were so lucky in our champions, really, when you think back."

With Fogarty's death, and Hill's and Lyndon Johnson's retirements, the enormous progress in federal support of library programs began to decline. While the seventies would see a continuation of most of the federal programs, the appropriations levels would remain relatively constant. In terms of the increase in inflation, a plateau on appropriations for library programs actually meant a decline in support. That was a problem which librarians and their allies, heady with their success of the sixties, never completely resolved.

Chapter 8

The Nixon Years to the Present (1969-81)

The 1970s saw the unfolding of the Nixon administration's determination to reduce federal expenditures for education and libraries, the creation of the National Commission on Libraries and Information Science, and the first White House Conference on Library and Information Services. During this decade, the Library Services and Construction Act was amended five times. Finally, it was a decade of studies and evaluations of the effectiveness of LSCA and other library programs, which saw the introduction of a new National Library bill. This proposed legislation may have within it the seeds of a law that might replace the Library Services and Construction Act, although it is too early to tell. It is beyond the scope of this report, which focuses on the origins of the original Library Services Act and its transformation into the Library Services and Construction Act in 1964, to discuss this period or these topics in depth. However, the participants in our review of the past twenty-five years of the Library Services Act have provided us a number of insights into the events of the early 1970s.

Commenting, in our sessions in Alexandria, on the Nixon presidency and its impact on libraries, referring particularly to his predilection for calling for zero funding for libraries, and the battles waged over his impounding of funds appropriated for libraries by Congress, Eileen Cooke stated "I think we have the basis of another two-hour tape, if we get into impoundment."

A brief discussion of the first year of the Nixon administration and the battle over the first appropriations bill for libraries and education is, nevertheless, indicative of the tenor of Nixon's entire administration as regards libraries and the beginning of his attempts at impoundment. Further, the legislative process involved in the adoption of the five amendments to the Library Services and Construction Act is given, even though these events were not discussed in any detail by the participants in our sessions.

Except for the first six months, Bessie Moore has served as Vice-Chairman of the National Commission on Libraries and Information Science since its establishment in 1970 under President Nixon. Based upon the success of the hearings conducted by the National Advisory Commission on Libraries, she says, the permanent commission, NCLIS, chose to hold hearings around the country in the early 1970s. She recalls,

> Sometimes a headline, if you have good story and if it's controversial, it will get everybody to read it. This happened to us in Portland, Oregon. The reporter was doing his best to understand what the Commission was all about. He asked all these questions: 'What would we be doing? Who should select books? Do we have anything to do with this?' Of course, we went into great explanations, that is Chairman Burkhardt did. Next morning, when the *Oregonian* was published, the big headline said, 'Would You Like for Richard Nixon to Be Your Librarian?' It was a very good story and I can assure you everyone read it.

With Bessie's story in mind, we entitle the following section:

"WOULD YOU LIKE FOR RICHARD NIXON TO BE YOUR LIBRARIAN?"

On January 15, 1969, President Johnson sent his 1970 budget message to Congress. The budget reflected the program priorities of the outgoing administration. Among the funds requested for programs beginning July 1, 1969, were $202 million in appropriations for on-going library programs. The library programs were authorized for well over $500 million. For example, the budget recommendation included $49,894,000, the same appropriation as for 1969, for all titles of LSCA, whereas the library authorizations were for $116,000,000.

The ALA Washington Office described it, at the time, as a bare-bones budget with priorities placed on people rather than things. For example, the budget for ESEA Title II, for school library materials, was set for $42 million, whereas its authorization was $200 million. No funds were provided for instructional materials under NDEA Title III. Two-thirds of the budget outlays for elementary and secondary education were for grants to improve the academic achievement of disadvantaged children.

After President Richard M. Nixon assumed office on January 20, 1969, he asked the Bureau of the Budget to look for areas to cut in Johnson's proposed education budget. All areas in the education budget were cut. However, it seemed that library funds had been cut most drastically of all. At a budget briefing on April 15, 1969, John Venneman, Undersecretary of the Department of Health, Education, and Welfare gave the administration's position on federal aid to libraries. Reflecting the Bureau of the Budget's recommendations, he stated, "In the context of the total Federal program for education, special programs for books and equipment are considered low priority" (*ALA Washington Newsletter*, April 17, 1969, p. 1).

Indeed, Nixon's proposed revision cut 66 percent of the Johnson budget proposed for programs for library users. Looking at it another way, the library programs were being asked to absorb almost 25 percent of the cuts recommended for all of the activities under the U.S. Office of Education.

In response to the proposed cuts, an all-out campaign to secure full funding for educational programs, including those for libraries, was mounted by an alliance of organizations representing education interests. The American Library Association joined several other groups to establish the Emergency Committee for Full Funding of Education Programs. Their purpose was to

> demonstrate to the Congress that the funding of educational programs to the level established in the authorizing statutes is warranted, timely and proper. It intends to alert Congress and the country in time to avert the intolerable consequences of a cutback in the current Federal educational effort, as is proposed in the revised budget estimates. To this end, the Committee will coordinate, on a voluntary basis, the joint efforts of all components of education at every level—from preschool through postgraduate study—both public and private (*ALA Washington Newsletter*, May 28, 1969, p. 3).

Charlie Lee, who became the volunteer leader for the committee, believes that President Johnson had deliberately sent out the barest bones budget for educational programs and libraries that he could.

> As a good Democrat and a canny Senator, he was not averse to leaving a few field mines for his successor. And they fell for it. The first thing they did was to cut this stringent budget by $400 million. This catalyzed communities in terms of re-asserting to Congress that the people back home like, want, and need these programs. And the libraries were marching to the fore. Even to the floor of the U.S. House of Representatives, quite inadvertently, on the arm of Speaker John McCormack.

Gerrie Krettek in discussing the funding problem with Speaker McCormack had found herself on the House floor where the Speaker had walked as she was talking with him!

Throughout the Spring of 1969 the budget battle raged. Ironically, President Nixon issued a statement launching the twelfth annual National Library Week, for April 20 to 26, 1969, with the following metaphor,

> Libraries are the banks of our educational system. They yield rich dividends in knowledge and in wisdom. They are a summing-up of past achievement and a stimulant to future progress. Never have we had greater reason than this year to celebrate National Library Week. . . . The need to bring the benefits of better education to those who have been bypassed by existing programs is more imperative than ever. By extending their services throughout the communities of America, our libraries immeasureably advance our goal, and perform the highest public good. For these and all their selfless efforts to serve, I congratulate America's librarians— a dedicated profession of men and women who enrich their fellow citizens, their communities, and their country. (Signed) Richard Nixon (*ALA Washington Newsletter,* May 2, 1969).

A *Washington Post* editorial replied to the president, "The metaphor, however meritorious, was infelicitously timed. It was uttered just a day or two before the President announced savage slashes in the Federal library budget for libraries and library services. These banks, apparently are not going to have very much money in them. And so their 'dividends in knowledge and wisdom' may be correspondingly meager" (*Washington Post*, Wednesday, May 14, 1969, p. A16, reprinted in the *ALA Washington Newsletter*, May 28, 1969).

This editorial and innumerable others across the country were part of a national campaign to gain funding for library and educational programs. Sylvia Porter, the syndicated newspaper columnist, joined the fight as did the editors of the *Saturday Review*. On July 9, 1969, the American Library Trustee Association made a march on Washington following the ALA Conference which was held that year in Atlantic City. Over 100 community leaders, representing 33 states, met with more than 100 congressmen. The push for library funding also gained momentum from a newly formed group, the Emergency Committee for Full Funding of Education Programs. The marchers were assured of the support of Representative Daniel Flood (D-Pennsylvania), Chairman of the House HEW Appropriations Subcommittee, and Senator Ralph Yarborough (D-Texas), Chairman of the Senate Labor and Public Welfare Committee.

After three months of work, the united efforts by the Emergency Committee for Full Funding of Education Programs paid off on July 31, 1969, when the House voted 393 to 16 to approve a $17.6 billion 1970 HEW Appropriations bill with a $900 million budget increase for education. Of this amount, $77,685,000 was added for the three major library programs, LSCA, ESEA, and HEA. For LSCA the House restored funds to the level recommended in the Johnson budget, $49,894,000. However, the Senate refused to act on the appropriations legislation. Four months into the federal fiscal year, which began July 1, 1969, the Senate had not yet passed an HEW appropriations bill. Senator Lister Hill's legislative skill and power were sorely missed. The House initiated a continuing resolution (H.J. Res. 966) to provide funds until a regular HEW appropriations bill for 1970 passed both houses and was signed by the president on December 7, 1969.

Upon signing the continuing resolution, President Nixon, in a memorandum to the heads of executive departments and agencies, emphasized his intention not to spend funds appropriated over and above his April, 1969 budget estimates. He stated further that, "no commitments will be made to spend these additional appropriations until the Congress has completed action on all appropriations bills and revenue measures" (*ALA Washington Newsletter*, November 20, 1969, p. 1).

After two days of debate, the Senate passed, 88 to 4, H.R. 13111, the 1970 Labor-HEW Appropriations Act. A compromise bill agreed to by both houses was sent to President Nixon, who vetoed that bill on January 26, 1970, and his veto was sustained in the House on January 28, 1970. A two-thirds vote was required to override his veto, but Democrats could only muster a 226 to 191 majority. The budget fight continued into 1970.

On February 2, 1970, President Nixon transmitted his 1971 budget request to Congress. He recommended $2.5 million less for libraries in his 1971 budget than he did for 1970. More importantly, he again recommended zero funding for LSCA Title II, public library construction.

Finally, on March 4, 1970, the House voted, 324 to 55, to approve the Senate version of the HEW Appropriations bill. President Nixon signed the 1970 HEW Appropriations bill on March 5, 1970, nine months into the year for which the budget was intended. At the end of the struggle the LSCA appropriation stood at $43,266,250, which was $20 million more than President Nixon had requested for 1970, but $5 million less than had been proposed in the Johnson budget. Funds for LSCA Title II were $7,807,250 down from the 1969 appropriations level of $9,185,000, and down from the 1968 level of $18,185,000, and the 1967 appropriation of $40,000,000.

In August, 1970, President Nixon vetoed another education budget sent to him by Congress on the grounds that it was inflationary because it exceeded his budget recommendations by $453 million. On August 13, 1970, the House overrode the Nixon veto by a 289 to 114 vote, "the objections of the President to the contrary notwithstanding." The Senate vote on August 18 was 77 to 16. The LSCA appropriations for 1971 were $47,801,500 up by $4.5 million from 1970. Funds for LSCA Title II stood at $7,092,500, down $700,000 from 1970's appropriation.

On October 8, 1970, the Department of Health, Education, and Welfare announced that it would withhold a portion of the U.S. Office of Education funds for fiscal year 1971 (July 1, 1970-June 30, 1971), pending review of the Justice Department's opinion on mandatory spending. The arbitrary withholding of funds appropriated by Congress had been feared since enactment of the USOE appropriations in mid-August. Because the cutback in funds opposed the will of Congress, the House Education and Labor Committee, sitting as an Ad Hoc Subcommittee on Oversight on October 12, 1970, held a hearing on the funding and operation of education programs. From Terrel Bell, Acting Commissioner of Education, and James B. Cardwell, Assistant Secretary Comptroller, HEW, the Committee learned that HEW had been authorized to allocate only 91 percent of the funds appropriated for education. The balance was being withheld pending the resolution of the legal issues involved and departmental deliberations on an overall HEW spending plan for 1971. Cardwell also told the committee that the Office of Management and Budget would not impose any limitations on appropriations for Emergency School Assistance. "These items, together with other high priority legislative items, have been kept outside the ceiling," stated Cardwell (*ALA Washington Newsletter*, October 22, 1970, p. 2).

On October 22, 1970, HEW Secretary Elliot L. Richardson announced that all the funds which were distributed on the basis of statutory formulas (like LSCA) had been released at the level of the full appropriations approved by Congress. One exception to this blanket release of funds was that USOE released only $9.9 million (the President's budget request) of the $15,325,000 for HEA Title II-A, the academic library program (*ALA Washington Office. Urgent Memorandum*. October 22, 1970).

THE LIBRARY SERVICES AND CONSTRUCTION ACT AMENDMENTS OF 1970

On September 21, 1970, the Senate, by a vote of 63 to 0, unanimously passed S. 3318, the Library Services and Construction Act Amendments of 1970. The Senate hearings for the bill had been held on January 27, 1970. The bill consolidated the library services programs relating to the institutionalized and handicapped (Title IV A and B) with the Title I program. The total amount authorized for LSCA over the five-year extension of the act to June 30, 1976, added up to $1,143,130,000, the first billion-dollar authorization for the public library program. Senator

Claiborne Pell (D-Rhode Island), Chairman of the Education Subcommittee, explained the principal provisions of the legislation:

> The bill before us is a rather simple, straightforward measure which extends and improves an already excellent program for another five years. Some have questioned the reason for a five-year extension. Suffice it to say that the previous reauthorization of this program was for a five-year program, and that the Administration bill sent up to us, S. 3549, was also for a five-year period. It can be seen that the bill is a reasonable extension of present law. Except for Title I, which calls for more funds due to the consolidation, the levels for Fiscal Year 1972 remain the same as those already authorized for Fiscal Year 1971. For the four fiscal years following, the authorization is raised 5 per cent each year, actually, a figure less that the rate of inflation. (*ALA Washington Newsletter*, September 24, 1970).

The proposed Senate Amendments would also broaden Title I to include assistance for (1) special library services for disadvantaged persons; (2) strengthening state library agencies; and (3) assistance to strengthen metropolitan libraries as national or regional resource centers.

Emphasizing the widespread support and bi-partisan nature of LSCA, Senator Winston Prouty (R-Vermont), ranking minority member of the Education Subcommittee, said,

> I should like to commend the distinguished chairman of our subcommittee, Mr. Pell, for his guidance and leadership in crafting of this legislation, which is a substantial clarification and updating of a program which has served the Nation well since its enactment in 1956. Many of us here, as did I, had the opportunity to support the Library Services and Construction Act in its original form during the 84th Congress as member of this or the other body, or have had the opportunity to support the bills continuing and modifying the program enacted in subsequent Congresses. The bill before us merits similar support. (*ALA Washington Newsletter*, September 24, 1970, p. 2).

On November 24, 1970, the House Education and Labor Committee by a vote of 27 to 0 agreed to an expansion and five-year extension of LSCA (H.R. 19363) with a total authorization of $1,144,175,000. Brought up under suspension of the rules, as was LSA in 1960, the 1970 LSCA extension and amendments were passed by the House and finally approved by the Senate on December 15, 1970.

The bill, said the ALA Washington Office, represented a sound compromise between the original seven-title bill recommended by the American Library Association and the one-title bill proposed by the administration, which was seeking complete consolidation of the existing provisions in the law. The three titles brought forward under the 1970 LSCA Amendments were: (1) Title I—Library Services; (2) Title II—Public Library Construction; and (3) Title III—Interlibrary Cooperation.

President Nixon signed the bill into law (P.L.-91-600) on December 30, 1970. It was ironic that a bill with such widespread acceptance in the Congress, because of its successful operation, had taken nearly a year to win final passage. Also, that in the closing weeks of the session its chances for survival hung in the balance because other forces were attempting to use the legislation as a vehicle to pull through entirely unrelated legislation.

CHANGING OF THE GUARD AT THE ALA WASHINGTON OFFICE

LSCA and other library legislation clearly faced formidable opposition from the Nixon administration. At the close of that administration's first term, ALA lost one of its most effective staff members when Germaine Krettek retired on November 30, 1972. Julia Bennett's successor had led many good crusades for library support at the federal level. During her fifteen years as Director of the ALA Washington Office she had greatly extended and expanded the political consciousness of librarians throughout the country. Moreover, her record of accomplishment was impressive. David Clift, ALA Executive Director, who retired the same year, estimated that Congress had appropriated more than $1.25 billion for library programs during Krettek's tenure. Of this amount more than $460 million was for LSA and LSCA programs.

Krettek's good works had not gone unnoticed by the profession she served. Achievement awards had come from the University of Denver and Drexel, and an honorary degree from her alma mater, the College of St. Elizabeth. ALA conferred upon her the Joseph W. Lippincott Award for Distinguished Service to the Library Profession in 1969 and added its highest award, Honorary Membership, in 1973. In praising Gerrie Krettek's accomplishments, David Clift recalled his initial hope that she would stay five years in the Washington Office. What a loss libraries would have suffered if her tenure had been so short!

Yet Gerrie Krettek did not leave the American Library Association without a capable successor. She was succeeded by Eileen Cooke, who had been her Assistant Director in the Washington Office since 1964. Cooke's tasks would be more difficult than those of her two predecessors, as subsequent paragraphs in this book make clear. Yet she met the difficulties with the same kind of competence, dedication, and enthusiasm that had been such notable characteristics of Bennett and Krettek. Under Eileen Cooke's direction, the ALA Washington Office has continued its role of promoting the library cause before a variety of national associations, as well as in Congress and among the governmental agencies.

IMPOUNDMENT OF LIBRARY FUNDS (1973)

On January 29, 1973, President Nixon submitted to Congress his fiscal year 1974 Budget. The Library Services and Construction Act program was among the federal aid programs that Nixon proposed to terminate in 1974. The administration expressed the belief that libraries were essentially state and local government responsibilities. John F. Hughes, former Acting Associate Commissioner for the Bureau of Libraries and Learning Resources, the name assumed by the library unit in 1971, stated that "the administration has proposed termination of some programs because they are not successful. The library programs fall into a category of successful programs. Termination of federal funds does not signify a denigration of the programs" (quoted in James W. Fry, "LSA and LSCA, 1956-1973: Legislative History," *Library Trends*, July, 1975, p. 20). The administration suggested revenue sharing as an alternative to continuation of direct federal aid, since public libraries were eligible under provisions of P.L. 92-512.

Concern over the issue of the president's attempts to control federal spending by not allowing executive agencies to spend funds appropriated by Congress, that is, by "impounding" them, reached its height in early 1973. On January 2, 1973, the chairmen of fifteen major Senate committees and the Senate majority leadership joined in a friend-of-the-court brief in a case to challenge the president's power to impound federal highway trust funds. The case was on appeal to the Eighth Circuit from the U.S. District Court for the Western District of Missouri. Speaking for the Senate group, Senator Sam J. Ervin (D-North Carolina) said,

> This practice by the executive is contemptuous of the role of Congress in our tripartite system of government. The fact that the Senate Committee chairmen and majority leadership have joined together in this effort indicates how deeply Congress is concerned with maintaining its constitutional powers and prerogatives. All Americans should be greatly encouraged by this historic action, and I believe its significance will equal that of the actions of the Congress in refusing the President's court packing scheme in the 1930s. (*ALA Washington Newsletter*, Jan 5, 1973, p. 2).

On January 30, 1973, the Council of the American Library Association issued a resolution protesting President Nixon's repeated recommendations for zero funding for library programs and his practices of impounding or rescinding previously approved appropriations. The ALA resolution stated

> Whereas President Nixon proposes to end major grants-in-aid to libraries in FY1974; and
> Whereas this annihilation of needed and effective programs would result in de-

vastating reduction or elimination of services to millions of library users; and . . . libraries would suffer loss of urgently needed funds at a time when most libraries are already experiencing financial difficulty; and

Whereas the President twice vetoed the appropriations for the Departments of Labor and Health, Education, and Welfare in FY 1973, and as a result federally supported library programs are now entering the eighth month of the fiscal year with a great uncertainty and, in some cases, at near crisis level of reduced funds; and

. . . Whereas, by all these actions, the President has shown that he claims the right to dictate educational priorities for the nation, contrary to the mandate of Congress; Now Therefore Be It

Resolved that the American Library Association expresses its grave concern over these erosions of the constitutional powers of Congress in the determination of national priorities, and urges the Congress (1) to move quickly to enact the third Labor-HEW appropriations bill for FY 1973 and override another veto should it occur; and (2) to enact a FY 1974 appropriation for libraries adequate to meet the needs of all the people whose access to information is the key to effective participation in society and often the key to survival itself. (*American Libraries* 4 (April, 1973): 224.)

On June 26, 1973, the House rejected the president's recommendation of zero funding for library programs by passing H.R. 8877 by a vote of 347 to 58. The bill, introduced by Rep. Daniel Flood (D-Pennsylvania) included an appropriation of $58,709,000 for LSCA. On July 1, 1973, President Nixon signed P.L. 93-52, which was a continuing resolution allowing appropriations for library programs based on the appropriation levels provided in the House bill.

Concerning the impoundment battles of the early 1970s, Charlie Lee observed,

I must give the devil his due. There is a legal theory that the administration had which is a gray area of our constitutional law. But by two devices, first, through getting court decisions and getting money cleared some two-and-one-half years later, you got a little blip on your appropriations. Secondly, it led to the problem we are now facing this year and next year. And that is, the consequences of the new budget operations. Because the Budget Control Act [of 1974] had as Title II, impoundment language, which, while giving the president authority to impound, did so under a set of rules that gave, in effect, Congress ultimate authority over whether or not recision or deferral would be approved.

As part of the by-products of the conservatively supported action it was added to let Congress put controls on its own spending. This is the genesis of the first and second budget resolutions and the reconciliation process that ought to follow the second resolution. Instead of being arbitrarily, and as far as I can see, without legislative backing, applied to the first budget resolution, this armed the Budget Committee with the power to tell the authorizing committees to cut and to tell the appropriations committees to cut. . . . The reconciliation process is going to be something we are going to be facing in the current year [1982] just before March

31st. What is riding on it is the money you think you have under the third continuing resolution for this year.

Early in the discussion of impoundment Lee noted that "one of the documents that came up used the phrase 'executive prerogative.' Some of us who remembered the great and glorious revolution of 1688 wondered if we had gone back in time."[1]

One of the important factors in the ability of state library agencies to fight the impounding of funds by Nixon, said Elizabeth Hughey Arline, was the good relationship they had developed with attorneys general in the states—brought about by the administrative procedures in LSA and LSCA. When action was needed in the filing of court cases and class actions, which are still occurring in 1981, the attorneys general were eager to file suits for the funds in behalf of libraries.

Another critical issue in the battle between administrations and Congress, according to Charlie Lee, comes from the nature of LSCA as a state grant, state-planned program:

Charlie Lee:
A senator or representative can know how much his state is going to get, given certain levels of appropriations. With all due respect to the Office of Education, and subsequently, the Department of Education, what programs are they really interested in?

They are interested in the discretionary programs where *they* determine where the money goes. Not where Congress has determined where the money goes. As one senator from Texas, now no longer serving, said, as we came out of a conference, he would be damned if he would give the president of the United States, Democrat or Republican, a little black bag to buy the next election.

Ed Holley:
One could say that under the Nixon Administration, this series of administrative actions . . . had a decided effect not in just reducing or stabilizing appropriations but attempting to change that altogether.

I like your point, Charlie, that the administration was not very sympathetic to library programs because indeed they couldn't manipulate them to achieve their purposes. I sat on one of the advisory committees and fought with many of these individuals about what they were doing to change the clear intent of Congress with respect to some of the library legislation. Not this particular legislation but other legislation. We get back to what we started with in the original regulations and to the selling of the people in the legal end, who interpreted the language, to give the executive branch the authority to do what Congress never intended for them to do.

---

[1]Lee's reference is to the "Glorious Revolution" against the despotic ways of James II (1633-1701) which placed William of Orange and Mary on the English throne in 1689.

Charlie Lee:
   And the reverse side of that coin is the importance of people like Gerrie and Eileen when the legislation is under consideration. They must be able to advise the staff and the members what the implications of certain phrases are. And get the intent of Congress to do such and so to make it so unequivocally as to give the least leeway possible to interpretation on the part of the General Counsel.

ADDITIONAL AMENDMENTS TO LSCA
(1973, 1974, AND 1977)

Three amendments were added to LSCA during 1973 and 1974. The first came as a part of the Older Americans Comprehensive Services Amendments of 1973 (P.L. 93-29). Signed into law on May 5, 1973, this amendment added "Older Reader Services" as a new Title IV to LSCA, but the title was never funded. In practice, services to older Americans have been made a priority under the library services supported under LSCA Title I. Also in 1973, the definition of "public library" was enlarged to include research libraries, such as the New York Public Library, which met certain criteria to be eligible to receive LSCA funds. This amendment to LSCA was accomplished under the "National Endowment for the Arts and Humanities Amendments of 1973" (P.L. 93-133).

   In 1974, LSCA was amended under the "Education Amendments of 1974" (P.L. 93-380) to add program priority within LSCA for library services to areas of high concentrations of persons of limited English-speaking ability.

   The latest amendment to the Library Services and Construction Act was signed into law by President Jimmy Carter on October 7, 1977. This amendment, which extended LSCA through 1982, required that the states match federal funds spent for administration of the Act with state or non-federal funds, updated the base year for meeting maintenance of effort requirements for services to the handicapped and institutionalized, and added an emphasis on strengthening major urban resource libraries.

   Prior to the expiration of LSCA's authorization (1982), the Act was extended for another three years under the Omnibus Budget Reconciliation Act of 1981. The Budget Reconciliation Act was part of the Reagan administration's efforts to lower authorization levels for some 250 federal programs, including library programs. The LSCA Title I authorization was reduced from $150 million to $65 million per year. At the same time the administration sought cuts in actual appropriations as well as authorization levels, preliminary to the complete elimination of these programs from the federal budget.

   One month after passage of the Reconciliation Act, in September, 1981, Congressman Paul Simon (D-Illinois) began a series of oversight hearings on the federal library programs. His action was intended to precede consideration of an act to extend LSCA in 1983. Thus the Budget Reconciliation Act has bought time for LSCA supporters but other battles loom ahead. Meanwhile, Congress has shown no inclination to eliminate any library programs despite the Reagan administration's recommendation of zero funding for most of them in 1982-83. Even so, the reduction in funding or stablized funding in a time of continuing inflation may well be undermining LSCA's effectiveness.

Chapter 9

Where Do We Go From Here?

Within this history we have discussed five decades of legislative activity by the American Library Association and twenty-five years of progress for American libraries under the auspices of the Library Services and Construction Act. Even its opponents agree that LSCA has been successful in achieving the original objectives. Indeed, for the last decade various administrative officials, both Democrat and Republican, have argued that federal legislation for libraries is no longer needed precisely *because* it has been successful.

When one looks at the historical record, examines the questions that opponents raised at the beginning, and compares them with the present questions, one notices that they have a familiar ring. For that reason we believe that this oral history project will be helpful, as the Congress and the current administration consider library legislation for the future. That all the participants believed the federal government has a role in supporting libraries is clear. That they believe the form of that role may change, while the principle remains the same, is equally clear. Their views may not be surprising but we will ignore them only at considerable risk to our society and its democratic values.

At the end of each videotaping session in Chapel Hill and in Alexandria, Virginia, moderator Ed Holley raised the question "Where do we go from here?" Because our participants have extensive political and professional experience, their answers seem an appropriate conclusion to this historical overview. Therefore we conclude our oral history with the final sections from the two tapes.

CONCLUDING STATEMENTS FROM THE CHAPEL HILL PARTICIPANTS

Moderator, Ed Holley:
   I think that we could say reasonably well that the Library Services [Act], subse-

quently the Library Services and Construction Act, at least for its first decade and a half gave enormous impetus to library development in this country and fulfilled the intentions of the originators. I think you said to me this morning, congressman, that it never was the intention to limit this [legislation] to rural libraries but that was just the first part of it and it was to subsequently expand.

I think it is . . . important to say that there was strong support from both sides of the aisle. We haven't mentioned George Aiken here but we should certainly not forget him. There are a lot of people we should mention and they were all important in helping the library cause.

I guess the question that has been raised by this administration and one that requires a great deal of thought on the part of us is, as Mrs. Moore said in the previous hour, we are again raising the question of what is the appropriate federal role for libraries. Is there a federal role for libraries?

We answered that question positively in this country in the sixties. We stabilized our commitment in the seventies.

And now the real question facing us at the end of the first twenty-five years of the Act's existence, is "Where do we go from here?"

What do we do next in terms of supporting libraries?

We have three minutes. One last word. We will go around.

Emerson Greenaway:

Well, I think we need a new act. This should take many scenes and a good scenario because we can become so mesmerized by what we did in the last quarter of a century that we will miss what's going on now and not get the kind of support that is necessary to provide service to people. I think that one of the things that has made the library program so acceptable nationwide is that we haven't gone out and gotten increased salaries for librarians, we have gone out to get more books to people, and more information to people. This is, I think, the key.

Evelyn Day Mullen:

I believe with Emerson that we need a new, a completely new act, because the other has gotten so verbose and involved that it has to be clarified. One of my feelings in retirement is that this emphasis on interlibrary cooperation to make all the resources of the libraries in the state or area available to all the people is one of the important approaches that we should make. There are more new ways all the time with all the electronic developments but we shouldn't just depend on those. There are other ways of doing it.

Bessie Moore:

I think we do have to have a new act. But I think we have got to get the librarians and the library advocates familiar with some statistics about some things happening right now. For example, if 54 percent of the Gross National Product is concerned with information, it's very foolish for the government to put its head in the sand and say that we have no business there.

Germaine Krettek:

I agree with you and I think that we need to get together as librarians and the users of libraries. And, of course, that was one of the intents of the White House Conference on Libraries. It has to be determined from what are the needs on both sides.

Carl Elliott:

I would say that the great need right now is to have a hard-hitting elastic organization that will go out and lobby day and night, in and out, for increased funds for the Library Services Act and any other act that might take its place. It ought to be done by individuals. It shouldn't be done by book publishers and book sellers and people who have axes to grind about the thing. But somehow or other we have got to get some funds to do a continuing lobbying job.

I don't mean to take the place of what ALA is doing. I mean somebody who can go into the highways and by-ways like we did twenty-five years ago and seek these votes and round them up to strengthen our position as library folks in the United States.

There is no question but that there is a serious competition for these public funds. I get the feeling that with the small office that ALA has and with the small office that everybody else has and the conflicting ideas that are going around from the book companies and the electronics people and all of that that there is a great need for real lobbying. Real hard-nose lobbying.

Ed Holley:

We are now out of time. I want to thank all of you for sharing with us. . . . people in the future [will also] thank you.

CONCLUDING STATEMENTS FROM THE ALEXANDRIA, VIRGINIA, PARTICIPANTS

Moderator, Ed Holley:

We are concluding our discussion of the Library Services and Construction Act. We have discussed its history, its development, its period of flourishing, its period of stability, and now I have asked our panelists to discuss with us, "Where do we go from here?"

The same role, the same questions of the appropriate federal role in library services and library support are being raised again as they were in the early fifties when the original Library Services Act legislation was introduced and subsequently passed and signed by the president on June 19, 1956. I want to pose for the panel, in the light of our discussion this afternoon and all of the previous records that we have examined individually and collectively, What is the federal role in library legislation?

Is there, indeed, a federal role in library legislation? Is the federal role in supporting education and libraries a limited role or is it a broader role and where do you think we are going from here?

I would like to turn again to my colleague, Eileen Cooke, as the first of the panelists, and perhaps the person with the best current insight into what is happening, and ask her. Where are we going? Why do we need continued federal legislation in support of libraries? What new and different directions do you see us moving in as we face the eighties?

Eileen Cooke:

I think, that as you might guess, there definitely is a federal role. In fact, as I have been sitting here listening to the previous discussion, I have seen that we are going through cycles. The first legislation was aimed at rural areas. When it was extended to take the population cap off, funding was increased to include the cities. Now we have come full cycle. We know that libraries provide important services; but if we are going to move into a new age, to accelerate the dissemination of information, we are going to have to take advantage of the new technologies and that calls for networks to take advantage of satellites, etc. And that cannot be done by the separate states. We really have to have some federal assistance to make this overarching pulling together of resources possible.

Ed Holley:

You are talking about large sums of capital acquisitions too, in terms of the technology.

Eileen Cooke:

Yes, as seed money. I think we have proven so well that the LSCA federal grant program has provided good seed money for generating better state support, better recognition, better local support.

Charlie Lee:

One political point, if I may, it is that [if] there is one star in our constitutional firmament, it is that no Congress can bind its successors. So the federal role in the future will be what the people elected by your constituents determine it will be.

Eileen Cooke:

One of the things I wanted to pick up on was a fact you mentioned early on in the very first tape—the importance of the grass roots input. That ALA had the support and sense of the people back home that library service was beneficial, similar, or complementary to a repeat of the county extension agency. You were working with people back at the state and local levels when this legislation was developed, and I believe that was one of the greatest assets we had, when the money was impounded, for example in 1973, or even back when many of the Great Society programs were being developed in the mid-sixties, Elementary and Secondary Education Act, Higher Education Act.

We already had in place that coalition at the national level and at the state and local level. I think we are going to have to revive and strengthen those grass roots ties because the need for strong grass roots support is very obvious in what is happening now. I don't know if we have mentioned it, but all of the library programs have been zeroed out in the eighty-three budget. So that does tend to focus the mind very sharply that there is a need for some action from the folks back home. We do need to justify a federal role if we believe there is one.

But we have many allies and what we are finding again, in this period of recession, is that people do tend to go back to the library and use it more heavily. They can't afford many of the materials. I was also impressed, as I listened to previous speakers, with the acknowledgement of the marvelous bi-partisan support which was developed over the years. That doesn't come and go with one administration or another. The support is there because the grass roots people believe in the library programs.

I think our programs are very basic and we are going to have to make that point particularly in view of the aspect that libraries are very labor intensive. Well-trained staff in adequate numbers is costly. To get around that problem we are going to have to take advantage of the new technologies. That definitely calls for large expenditures of money or very large donations on the part of the private sector by way of hardware and the materials, software, that can be used in libraries. Many people will come in that may not be print-oriented. They may need information in various formats and . . . we have the role. We're going to have to take over in the new cycle. In addition we may well be continuing many of the on-going activities; they are very basic.

Elizabeth Hughey Arline:

I seems to me that we have a strong initiative to build on from the Interlibrary Cooperation Title III of LSCA, which was a non-matching [program] . . . which can involve every type of library and information agency within a community, and [is] not limited there. [There are also] interstate compacts—nearly every state now has that for crossing state lines with distribution of information and materials.

We have the mechanism right here for what could become a national network, a national cooperative program, and I think it is very necessary in this period where even our third graders are into technology. They are learning how to operate many of these machines. They are learning how to utilize things that were never even in existence when we began working on this legislation.

We need to capitalize on the possibilities here and bring together all elements which can focus on providing information services and materials to people.

Ed Holley:

Would you say that philosophically our basis is that in a democracy, to use Mr. Jefferson's terms, you cannot be democratic and uneducated? That is, no democracy can survive on an illiterate populace (Arline: Right) and therefore education and the means to information in the information age represents a conscious national priority item rather than a local or state role. Therefore, we are going to have to take advantage of whatever means we can to look at this in national perspective.

We used to say that you can't have an illiterate black in Alabama and have sophisticated technology and all the rest of it, and have a democracy in which you expect everybody to participate. It goes back to the old idea that you can't vote democratically if you don't know what you are voting for. That is increasingly difficult, I realize, for a variety of reasons. It is a clash of philosophical principles, is it not?

It represents a very serious challenge to the events of the last thirty or forty years.

John Lorenz:

I would say that there is a federal role based upon our philosophy of equal opportunity. I think that has been pretty well established. And this [is an] information society in which one-third of our Gross National Product is related to education and information. And whereas access to information means equal opportunity and equal access to progress on the part of individuals as well as the society, that there is a federal role to accomplish that equal opportunity for access to information throughout our society.

Roger McDonough:

I almost find it unthinkable to contemplate a society where the federal government pulls back at this point in history from participating with the states and the counties and municipalities in a cooperative approach that will make all the information that we can put our hands on available cooperatively to all our citizens.

When mention was made that kids today are learning to use sophisticated learning equipment I thought of my wife, who is working with third grade children in the Princeton schools, and they are operating machinery that I don't know anything about. The state library when I became the head in 1947 didn't know what a data base was and it's now tied into one hundred plus different data bases and it is connected by telephone and other computer means to the entire country, including Washington. It's just unthinkable to me that we wouldn't have this fusion of federal, state, and local library-information-effort.

Paul Howard:

The way to destroy a program is to divide it. That's what this attempting to put the support back to the local level would do. It would divide it.

You wouldn't have the same library service in New York that you would have in Alabama.

The only progress our country has made has been through joint action. The difference between us and South America economically is because we had a continental market which was enhanced by the grants to the railroads and so on. The same thing [applies here]. We've got to have a continental market in our educational programs and our library programs. If we don't, why we will be divided and balkanized.

Charlie Lee:

Thinking back to what we started with today, the precursor legislation, which while not enacted, nevertheless served as a rallying point that led later on to a successful conclusion. One of the Great Society programs that was passed, but never funded, Networks for Knowledge, inherently had within it the germ of what we are talking about here.

I think we ought to look at all our educational legislation as an unfinished mosaic where every part has an important and crucial place and role to play.

We can tear it down from time to time but only if we rebuild it greater in the future. That is what I meant. You mentioned one-third of the Gross National Product. Demographically, teachers and taught of all ages are one-third of the population. Given those who are affected by those teaching and taught, you're well over the majority required for political action.

Since every generation faces challenges that have been met in the past by predecessors, you will face challenges decade after decade into the future. We need only lose hope if we change the fundamental basis by which we arrive at societal decisions. And that, I think, is the essence of what Jefferson was getting at: that a democracy requires a literate population.

Eileen Cooke:

Charlie reminded me of one of my favorite pieces of legislation, the Networks for Knowledge. Congress made it Title VIII of the Higher Education Act in the mid-sixties but never funded it and eventually repealed the program. It had a provision for preferential telecommunications rates which I have been saying we must pick up on because we have preferential postal rates to point to as a precedent, although they are finally being eroded with the overall increased postal costs and the reduction in the subsidy. I think this is something that libraries really need to provide, this linking, by using satellites, computerized data bases, and developing the cable library systems.

As you may know, in Denver ALA had the experiment with our public awareness program via satellite transmissions with sixty cable libraries picking it up and the National Library of Agriculture using an antenna dish receiver. If libraries are going to be able to take advantage of the new technology, this is one significant way the government could provide assistance.

If Congress and the U.S. government agencies have a federal telecommunications system—which they do—why not preferential (or subsidized) telecommunications rates for library services? That would be one way, without giving various grants to libraries, to really help provide this linking of library services.

John Lorenz:

Another way of looking at it is that equal access to education got this civilization to where it is today. It is going to be just as important in terms of the rate of change of society that equal access to information be available to all our citizenry in the future.

Ed Holley:

And that, at length, ties us back to the original Act and the forces that brought it into existence, does it not? That it *is* the attempt by all of us to try to find the materials that our citizens need for their education, for their recreation, for developing the quality of life. Perhaps it is important here in the State of Virginia, in 1982, to conclude with Mr. Jefferson's famous statement that "No republic can be ignorant and free."

And on that, I think, we take our stand.

***Panel*:**
  Amen.

BIBLIOGRAPHY

Several persons have told the story of the American Library Association's involvement with the federal government. Among those works generally acknowledged are Kathleen Molz, *National Planning for Library Service 1935 to 1975: From the National Plan to the National Program* (Columbia University, DLS dissertation, 1976) and *Federal Policy and Library Support* (1976), which approach the problem from a policy point of view; Hawthorne Daniel's *Public Libraries for Everyone: Growth and Development of Library Services in the U.S., Especially since the Passage of the Library Services Act* (1961), and James Healey's *John Fogarty: Political Leadership for Library Development* (1974). As the bibliographical record indicates, articles on federal legislation are extensive. The authors have found particularly helpful James Fry's "LSA and LSCA, 1956-1973: A Legislative History," *Library Trends*, July 1975, and Germaine Krettek's "Library Legislation, Federal," in the *Encyclopedia of Library and Information Science* 15:337-354 (1975). Earlier, and helpful, were the September 1955 issue of the *Wilson Library Bulletin*, which contained articles and formal statements of witnesses before the House subcommittee of the Committee on Education and Labor in 1955 and Germaine Krettek's "LSA, the Federal Government, and the Profession," in the Allerton Park Institute proceedings, *Impact of the Library Services Act: Progress and Potential* (1961). So useful were two compilations by the U.S. Office of Education, one on LSCA legislative chronology and the other on federal funding, that they have been included as appendices in this report. We should also mention an excellent scrapbook kept by Julia Bennett Armistead whose contents have been copied for our collections at UNC. Indeed, the Chapel Hill collection of material on LSCA will provide important data for those who wish to pursue further research in LSCA or related topics, and they will be made available to qualified researchers.

What follows is an extensive bibliography developed for this oral history project. The bibliography includes articles and books, arranged chronologically, with relevant government documents at the end of each section. We trust that this bibliographical record will provide an important beginning point for more detailed study of the federal role in library development.

LSA/LSCA BIBLIOGRAPHY

I. Early Efforts for Library Legislation (1935-1950)

American Library Association. *Washington Newsletter.* v. 1- 1949-.

American Library Association. Council. "Report of the Denver Conference, Federal Aid for Libraries," *Library Journal* 40 (September 15, 1935): 706-771.

American Library Association. Council. "Report of the May 11th Meeting," *ALA Bulletin* 30 (August 1938): 309-311.

Barker, Tommie Dora. *Libraries of the South: A Report on Developments, 1930-1935.* Chicago: American Library Association, 1936.

"Chronological Summary of Federal Aid to Libraries," *ALA Bulletin* 32 (September 1938): 635-636.

Compton, Charles H. "Federal Aid to Libraries—Our Present Opportunity." *ALA Bulletin* 32 (December 1938): 1011-1072.

Douglas, Emily Taft. "Rural Libraries in America," *ALA Bulletin* 40 (September 1946): 269-272.

Elliott, Ella M. "Federal Relations of the American Library Association, 1930-1940." Unpublished Master's Thesis. University of Chicago, 1946.

"Federal Aid Bill Before Congress," *ALA Bulletin* 32 (May 1938): 309-322.

Federal Aid for Libraries. (Pamphlet) Chicago: American Library Association, 1939.

Fielder, Clara M. "Library Demonstration Bill Introduced," *ALA Bulletin* 43 (February 1949): 76.

Gregory, Ruth W. "The Library Development Fund," *ALA Bulletin* 40 (October 1946): 308-309.

Healey, James S. *John Fogarty: Political Leadership for Library Development.* Metuchen, N.J.: Scarecrow Press, 1974.

Healey, James S. "The Emergence of National Political Leadership for Library Development: The Case of Representative John E. Fogarty." DLS Dissertation. Columbia University, 1973.

Howard, Paul. "Legislation before Congress," *District of Columbia Libraries* 20 (October 1948-January 1949): 5-6.

Joeckel, Carleton B. "Federal Relations to Libraries," *ALA Bulletin* 29 (February 1935): 60-63.

Joeckel, Carleton B. "The New Federal Library Agency," *ALA Bulletin* 30 (July 1936): 529.

Joeckel, Carleton B., and Winslow, Amy. *A National Plan for Public Library Service*. Chicago: American Library Association, 1948.

"Libraries and Federal Aid," *ALA Bulletin* 30 (May 1936): 427-471.

"Library Demonstration Bill Defeated in the House," *Library Journal* 75 (April 1, 1950): 548.

Mohrhardt, C. M. "Library Demonstration Bill," *Michigan Librarian* 15 (March 1949): 5.

Molz, Redmond Kathleen. "National Planning for Library Service, 1935 to 1975: From the National Plan to the National Program." DLS Dissertation. Columbia University, 1976.

Newman, William Austin. "Congress and the Public Library: Legislative Proposals and Action for Federal Assistance, 1938 to 1956." DLS Dissertation. Case Western Reserve University, 1980.

"Prospects for Library Legislation in a Defense Economy," *Library Journal* 75 (November 15, 1950): 1975-1976.

"Report of the American Library Association Committee on Federal Relations." Carleton B. Joeckel, Chairman, *ALA Bulletin* 30 (January 1936): 34-35; 30 (May 1936): 427-471; 30 (September 1937): 560-561; 32 (September 1938): 634-636; 33 (September 1939): 606-615.

"Report of the American Library Association Committee on Federal Relations," Forrest Spaulding, Chairman, *ALA Bulletin* 34 (April 1940): 240.

Ring, Daniel F. (ed.) *Studies in Creative Partnership: Federal Aid to Public Libraries During the New Deal*. Metuchen, N.J.: Scarecrow Press, 1980.

Schenk, Gretchen K. "Stronger Than the Legislature," *Washington State Library News Notes* 25 (July 1949): 95-99.

Spaulding, Forrest B. "Hold Federal Aid Bill Till Next Year," *ALA Bulletin* 34 (April 1940): 240.

"Summer Reading from the Congressional Record for March 9, 1950; or, Why the Public Library Service Demonstration Bill Failed," *Arizona Librarian* 7 (Summer 1950): 16-18.

Thompson, C. Seymour. "The Abdication of the A.L.A.," *Library Journal* 40 (May 1, 1935): 368-372.

Toomey, Mary C. "Federal Relations Notes from the Midwinter Conference," *ALA Bulletin* 41 (February 1947): 45-47.

Vitz, Carl. *A Federal Library Agency and Federal Library Aid.* Chicago: American Library Association, 1935.

Vitz, Carl. "A.L.A. Federal Relations Fund; Why a Special Campaign?" *ALA Bulletin* 39 (January 1945): 19.

Wilson, Louis Round. *The Geography of Reading.* Chicago: American Library Association, 1938.

* * *

Howard, Paul. "Statement of Paul Howard, Director, National Relations Office, American Library Association, May 29, 1946." U.S. Congress. Senate. Committee on Labor and Public Welfare. *Public Library Service Demonstration Bill; Hearings before Subcommittee on S. 1920.* 79th Congress. 2nd Session. 1946, pp. 3-9.

Joeckel, Carleton B. *Library Service.* Prepared for the Advisory Committee on Education, Staff Study No. 11. Washington, D.C.: Government Printing Office, 1938.

U.S. Congress. Senate. Committee on Labor and Public Welfare. *Public Library Service Demonstration Bill. Hearings before a Subcommittee on S. 1920; A Bill to Provide for the Demonstration of Public Library Service in Areas Without Such Service or with Inadequate Library Facilities.* 79th Congress. 2nd Session. 1946 (Held May 29, 1946).

U.S. Congress. Senate. Committee on Labor and Public Welfare. *Public Library Service Demonstration Bill.* Report to accompany S. 1920. 79th Congress. 2nd Session. 1946. Senate Report No. 1575. (June 21 [Legislative day, March 5], 1946).

U.S. Congress. Senate. Committee on Labor and Public Welfare. *Demonstration of Public-Library Service. Hearings before a Subcommittee on S. 48; A Bill to Provide for the Demonstration of Public-Library Service in Areas Without Such Service or with Inadequate Library Facilities.* 80th Congress. 1st Session. 1947 (Held May 16, 1947).

U.S. Congress. House. Committee on Education and Labor. *Demonstration of Public Library Service. Hearings before Subcommittee No. 1 on H.R. 2465; A Bill to Provide for the Demonstration of Public Library Service in Areas Without Such Service or with Inadequate Library Facilities.* 80th Congress. 1st Session. 1947 (Held December 9 and 10, 1947).

U.S. Congress. Senate. Committee on Labor and Public Welfare. *Public Library Service Demonstration Bill.* Report to accompany S. 130. 81st Congress. 1st Session. 1949. Senate Report No. 2 (January 24, 1949).

U.S. Congress. House. Committee on Education and Labor. *Public Library Demonstration Bill.* Report to accompany H.R. 874.

81st Congress. 2nd Session. 1950. House Report No. 1574 (February 2, 1950).

U.S. Congress. House. Committee on Rules. Consideration of H.R. 874. Report to accompany H.Res. 481. 81st Congress. 2nd Session. 1950. House Report No. 1667 (February 20, 1950).

U.S. Congress. House. "Public Library Demonstration Bill, H.R. 874" (Floor Debate and Final Vote). 81st Congress. 2nd Session. March 9, 1950. *Congressional Record*, Vol. 96 Pt. 6:3122-3142.

U.S. Congress. House. Representative John F. Kennedy speaking against the Public Library Demonstration Bill. 81st Congress. 2nd Session. March 9, 1950. *Congressional Record*, Vol. 96 Pt. 6:3129, 3133.

U.S. Congress. House. Representative Carl Perkins speaking for the Public Library Demonstration Bill. 81st Congress. 2nd Session. March 9, 1950. *Congressional Record*, Vol. 96 Pt. 6:3129-30.

II. Library Services Act (1951-1956)

Agria, John J. "The American Library Association and the Library Services Act." Ph.D. Dissertation. University of Chicago, 1966.

Allott, Gordon L. "Senatorial Support of Library Services Bill," *Colorado Library Association Bulletin* No. 46 (September 1956): 33-34.

American Library Association. Federal Relations Committee. "Minutes of Open Meeting on Federal Legislation," January 29, 1957.

American Library Association. Special Committee on Federal-State Relations. *The Federal Government and the Public Library*. Chicago: American Library Association, 1954.

Bayless, J. E. "Can We Use $239,598?" *California Librarian* 17 (April 1956): 115-116+.

Bennett, G. "Library Services Act in Colorado," *Colorado Library Association Bulletin* No. 47 (December 1956): 11-27.

Bennett, Julia. "ALA Washington Notes—Library Service Act Public Law 597," *Wilson Library Bulletin* 31 (September 1956): 80.

Bennett, Julia. "An Anniversary," *District of Columbia Libraries* 26 (April 1955): 7-10.

Bennett, Julia. "A Cooperative Venture," *Public Libraries* 7 (December 1953): 11.

Bennett, Julia. "Editorial," *ALA Bulletin* 50 (July-August 1956): 406-408.

Bennett, Julia. "Editorial," *ALA Bulletin* 51 (February 1957): 72+.

Bennett, Julia. "Federal Legislation," *American Library Annual for 1955-1956.* New York: Bowker, 1955.

Bennett, Julia. "Federal Legislation," *American Library Annual for 1956-1957.* New York: Bowker, 1956.

Bennett, Julia. "Footnotes to the Library Services Act," *Saturday Review* 40 (June 22, 1957): 14.

Bennett, Julia. "A Librarian on Capitol Hill," *Mountain-Plains Library Quarterly* 1 (Fall 1956): 5-8.

Bennett, Julia. "Library Service for Rural Americans," *Libri* 7, No. 2-3 (1957): 167-172.

Bennett, Julia. "Library Services Bill," *Library Journal* 79 (January 1, 1954): 28-29.

Bennett, Julia. "Library Services Bill," *Library Journal* 80 (March 15, 1955): 614.

Bennett, Julia. "Library Services Bill," *Wilson Library Bulletin* 30 (September 1955): 81.

Bennett, Julia. "Library Services Bill-H.R. 2840: Time for Action," *ALA Bulletin* 49 (September 1955): 393-394.

Bennett, Julia. "Our Federal Relations," *Library Journal* 79 (March 1, 1954): 420.

Bennett, Julia. "Practicing What We Preach," *Public Libraries* 6 (November 1952): 79-84.

Bennett, Julia. "Questions and Answers on the Library Services Bill," *Library Journal* 78 (November 1, 1953): 1894-1895.

Bennett, Julia. "Questions and Answers on the Library Services Bill," *Library Journal* 78 (November 15, 1953): 1994-1995.

Bennett, Julia. "Questions and Answers on the Library Services Bill," *Library Journal* 78 (December 15, 1953): 2162-2163.

Bennett, Julia. "Working for Libraries in the Nation's Capital," *The Quotarian* December 1954, pp. 3 +

Bennett, Julia, and Dunbar, Ralph. "How Many and How Much— Some Statistical Facts," *ALA Bulletin* 48 (October 1954): 520-525.

Bequette, Mrs. N. L. "Library Legislation on the National Level," *Washington State Library News Bulletin* 21 (September-October 1954): 181-18.

Bete, Channing L. "Why I Am for the Library Services Bill," *ALA Bulletin* 49 (June 1955): 263.

Bete, Channing L. "Will the Library Services Bill Pass?" *Library Journal* 81 (January 15, 1956): 141-143.

Blanchard, E. A. "Library Trustees and the Library Services Bill," *Illinois Libraries* 35 (March 1953): 117-119.

Brown, Karl. "Tentative State Plans for Federal Aid," *Library Journal* 81 (December 15, 1956): 2890-2892.

"California and the Library Services Bill," *News Notes of California Libraries* 51 (July 1956): 403-406.

Clift, David H. "Looking Ahead," *Public Libraries* 10 (December 1956): 81-83 +.

Daniel, Hawthorne. *Public Libraries for Everyone; The Growth and Development of Library Services in the United States, Especially Since the Passage of the Library Services Act.* New York: Doubleday & Company, 1961.

Dunbar, Ralph M. "Public Library Extension; Legal Control and Structure," *Public Libraries* 10 (May 1956): 28-30.

Exton, Elaine. "Library Needs Catch Capital Spotlight," *American School Board Journal* 133 (July 1956): 45-46 +

Farrell, Sally J. "Federal Legislation of Interest to Librarians," *Louisiana Library Association Bulletin* 15 (Spring 1952): 48-49.

"Federal Aid," *New Hampshire Public Library Bulletin* 52 (September 1956): 25-26.

"Federal Library Service Bill," *Kansas Library Bulletin* 20 (March 1951): 13-14.

"Four States Look at the Library Services Bill: Michigan, New Mexico, Georgia, Washington," *Public Libraries* 6 (November 1952): 91-94.

Fry, James W. "LSA and LSCA, 1956-1973: A Legislative History," *Library Trends* 24 (July 1975): 7-26.

Fyan, Loleta D. "Library Services Act; The Role of PLD in Implementation," *Public Libraries* 10 (December 1956): 86-88 +.

Galick, V. G. "Public Law 597; The Library Services Act and How It Works," *Bay State Librarian* 46 (Autumn 1956): 9-12.

"Getting Ready for the Library Services Bill; A Panel Discussion," *South Dakota Library Bulletin* 42 (January-March, 1956): 113-118. Also appeared in *Idaho Librarian* 8 (April 1956): 15-21.

"Grants-in-Aid for Library Services," *Social Service Review* 30 (December 1956): 457-458.

Hacker, Harold S. "Case in Point," *New York Library Association Bulletin* 3 (October 1955): 72-75.

Hamlin, Arthur T. "Library Services Act," *College and Research Libraries* 17 (September 1956): 428-429.

Harris, B. "Bookman's View of the Library Services Act," *Colorado Library Association Bulletin* No. 47 (December 1956): 28-30.

"Highlights of Library Legislation before the U.S. Congress," *Vermont Library Bulletin* 51 (June 1955): 2-4.

Howard, Paul. "Associations and United States Legislation," *Library Trends* 3 (January 1955): 279-289.

Kee, S. Janice. "Library Services Act," *Wisconsin Library Bulletin* 52 (November-December 1956): 262-264.

Kennedy, F. M. "Library Service Bill," *Oklahoma Librarian* 1 (Summer 1951): 3+.

"Knowledge Is Power; A Summary of the Library Services Bill," *ALA Bulletin* 46 (January 1952): 21-24.

Leigh, Carma. "Remembrances on the Occasion of LSCA's 25th Anniversary," Adapted from remarks made at the President's Program of the American Library Association Conference, San Francisco, June 29, 1981, *ALA Yearbook, 1982*. Chicago: American Library Association, 1982, pp. 284-285.

Leigh, Robert D. "Changing Concepts of the Public Library's Role," *Library Quarterly* 27 (October 1957): 223-234.

"Library Services Act," *ALA. Washington Newsletter* 8 (October 17, 1956): 1-3.

"Library Services Act; Public Law 597—84th Congress, Chapter 407—Second Session, H.R. 2840," *American Library Annual for 1956-57*. New York: Bowker, 1956.

"Library Services Act," *Library Occurrent* 18 (September 1956): 235-237.

"Library Services Act in Michigan," *Michigan Library News* 16 (Winter 1956): 3-4.

"Library Services Bill," *Library Journal* 77 (January 1, 1952): 12-14.

"Library Services Bill," *Minnesota Libraries* 16 (March 1951): 264.

"Library Services Bill," (Editorial) *New York Times*, 5 May 1956, sec. 2, p. 18.

"Library Services Bill," *Pennsylvania Library Association Bulletin* 11 (Fall 1955): 9.

"Library Services Bill," *South Dakota Library Bulletin* 41 (October-December 1955): 93-96.

"Library Services Bill," *Utah Library Association Newsletter* 18 (Spring 1956): 24.

"Library Services Bill and Other Legislation," *South Dakota Library Bulletin* 42 (January-March 1956): 111-112.

"Library Services Bill H.R. 2840, S. 205," *Michigan Librarian* 22 (March 1956): 22.

"Library Services Bill; What It Can Mean to You!" *Iowa Library Quarterly* 17 (April 1956): 179-180.

"Library Lobbyist Eats at Office—Sleeps, Too—When Book Bills Loom," *News-Sentinel* (Knoxville) September 15, 1954.

Lindquist, R. C. "Tell It to the Congressman," *Library Journal* 81 (January 1, 1956): 39-43.

Lindquist, R. C. "Our Bill Needs Our Help Today," *Public Libraries* 6 (June 1952): 43+.

Loizeaux, Marie D. "The Challenge Ahead; The Library Services Act Is Only the Beginning," *Wilson Library Bulletin* 31 (September 1956): 55-57.

Loizeaux, Marie D. "House of Representatives Passes Library Services Bill by Voice Vote, May 8, 1956," *Wilson Library Bulletin* 30 (June 1956): 757-758.

Loizeaux, Marie D. "Library Services Bill in the Making," *Wilson Library Bulletin* 30 (September 1955): 41-61.

Malmberg, Marjorie. "Library Services Bill," *ALA Bulletin* 45 (March 1951): 100-101.

Malmberg, Marjorie. "Library Services Bill," (another article) *Public Libraries* 5 (February 1951): 4+.

Malmberg, Marjorie. "Boys on the Hill; The Strategy of Working with the Legislators," *Massachusetts Library Association Bulletin* 41 (October 1951): 53-57.

Melcher, Frederic G. "As the Library Service Bill Begins to Have Effect," *Publishers' Weekly* 170 (December 17, 1956): 2579.

"Michigan State Board for Libraries Law," *Library Journal* 78 (December 1, 1953): 2085-2086.

Ottemiller, John H. "Library Services Bill; Another Chance," *ALA Bulletin* 47 (March 1953): 99+.

Richards, John S. "Library Services Bill," *Library Journal* 80 (June 1955): 1431-1435.

Roberts, Mrs. L. B. "Library Services Bill a Reality," *Alabama Librarian* 7 (July 1956): 20.

Schenk, Gretchen K. *County and Regional Library Development.* Chicago: American Library Association, 1954.

Schenk, Gretchen K. "Founding Fathers' Oversight," *Pacific Northwest Library Association Quarterly* 15 (January 1951): 73-81.

Sinclair, D. "Library Services and California Library Development," *News Notes of California Libraries* 51 (October 1956): 496-500.

Thornton, E. "What Are the Provisions of the Library Services Bill?" *Focus on Indiana Libraries* 10 (May 1956): 3-4.

* * *

Beach, Fred F., Dunbar, Ralph M., and Will, Robert F. "The State and Publicly Supported Libraries: Structure and Control at the State Level." (U.S. Office of Education, Misc. No. 24) Washington, D.C.: U.S. Dept. of Health, Education, and Welfare, Office of Education, 1956.

Richards, John S. "Statement of John Richards, Director, Seattle Public Library, Seattle, Washington, and President-Elect, American Library Association," U.S. Congress. House. *Federal Aid for Library Service in Rural Areas, Hearings before a Subcommittee of the Committee on Education and Labor.* 84th Congress. 1st Session. May 25, 1955, pp. 22-58.

U. S. Commission on Intergovernmental Relations. Study Committee on Federal Responsibility in the Field of Education. *A Study Committee Report on Federal Responsibility in the Field of Education.* Submitted to the Commission on Intergovernmental Relations. Washington, D.C.: Government Printing Office, 1955. (Also known as the Kestnbaum Report).

U.S. Congress. Senate. Committee on Labor and Public Welfare. *Promoting the Further Development of Public Library Service in Rural Areas.* Report to accompany S. 1452. 82nd Congress. 1st Session. 1951. Senate Report No. 775 (September 17 [Legislative day, September 13], 1951—Ordered to be printed).

U.S. Congress. House. *Library Services in Rural Areas. Hearings before a Subcommittee of the Committee on Education and Labor on H.R. 5195; A Bill to Promote the Further Development of Public Library Service in Rural Areas.* 82nd Congress. 2nd Session. 1952 (Hearings held at Washington, D.C., April 1 and 2, 1952).

U.S. Congress. House. Committee on Education and Labor. *Federal Aid for Library Service in Rural Areas. Hearings before a Subcommittee on Bills to Promote the Further Development of Public Library Service in Rural Areas.* 84th Congress. 1st Session. 1955 (Hearings held at Washington, D.C., May 25, 26, and 27, 1955).

U.S. Congress. House. Committee on Education and Labor. *Federal Aid for Library Service in Rural Areas.* Report to accompany H.R. 2840. 84th Congress. 1st Session. 1955. House Report No. 1587 (July 29, 1955).

U.S. Congress. House. Committee on Rules. Consideration of H.R. 2840. Report to accompany H. Res. 479. 84th Congress. 2nd Session. 1956. House Report No. 2020 (April 19, 1956).

U.S. Congress. House. Floor Debate on Library Services Act. 84th Congress. 2nd Session. May 8, 1956. *Congressional Record*, Vol. 102, Pt. 6: 7683-7711.

U.S. Congress. Senate. Committee on Labor and Public Welfare. *Library Services. Hearings before the Subcommittee on Education on S. 205; A Bill to Promote the Further Development of Public Library Service in Rural Areas and H.R. 2840; An Act to Promote the Further Development of Public Library Service in Rural Areas.* 84th Congress. 2nd Session. 1956 (Held May 23, 1956).

U.S. Congress. Senate. Committee on Labor and Public Welfare.

Library Services Act. Report to accompany H.R. Res. 2840. 84th Congress. 2nd Session. 1956. Senate Report No. 2067 (May 24, 1956).

U.S. Congress. Senate. Committee on Appropriations. *Hearings on Second Appropriations Bill.* 84th Congress. 2nd Session. 1956. (Harold Tucker testimony for ALA July 20, 1956). (Bill passed Senate July 25, 1956).

U.S. Congress. Joint Conference Committee on the Second Appropriations Bill. 84th Session. 2nd Session August 15, 1956.

U.S. President. *Public Papers of the President Dwight David Eisenhower.* "Message upon Signing the Library Services Bill-June 19, 1956." Washington, D.C.: Government Printing Office, 1958, p. 557.

U.S. *Statutes at Large.* Vol. 70. Public Law 84-597. *Library Services Act.* (Provided Public Library Services for Rural Areas Only). 84th Congress. 2nd Session. June 19, 1956.

U.S. *Statutes at Large.* Vol. 70. Organic Act. (Added Guam to List of Territories). 84th Congress. 2nd Session. August 1, 1956.

III. Library Services Act (1957-1960)

American Library Association. Federal Relations Committee. "Minutes of Open Meeting on Federal Legislation, January 29, 1957," ALA. *Washington Newsletter* 9 (March 6, 1957): Supplement, pp. 1-3.

Barker, Tommie D. "Plans of SELA States for Use of Funds under the Library Services Act (Public Law 597, 84th Congress, 2nd Session)," *Southeastern Librarian* 7 (Fall 1957): 75-83 +.

Bennett, Julia "Footnotes to the Library Services Act," *Saturday Review* 40 (June 22, 1957): 14.

Bennett, Julia "The Library Services Act—The First Year," *Wilson Library Bulletin* 32 (September, 1957): 39-43.

Bennett, Julia "Washington Report-Appropriations," *ALA Bulletin* 51 (November 1957): 785-786.

Bennett, Julia, and McCaskill, James. "ALA and NEA—Partners in Federal Relations," *ALA Bulletin* 51 (April 1957): 282-285.

Blasingame, Jr., Ralph. "LSA and the Future," in Strout (ed.), *Impact of the Library Services Act: Progress and Potential* (1961) pp. 87-92. See entry under Strout.

"Books, USA," (Prepared by Library Services Branch in cooperation with *School Life* staff). *School Life* 42 (December 1959):12-13.

Boord, Miller. "A University Cooperates," *Wilson Library Bulletin* 33 (May 1959): 651.

Brown, Karl. "Congress and the LSA," *Library Journal* 84 (October 15, 1959): 2903-2904.

Brown, Karl. "Library Services Act," *American Library and Book Trade Annual*. New York: Bowker, 1958, pp. 121-131; 1959, pp. 80-87; 1960, pp. 113-126.

Brown, Karl (compiler). "Tentative Plans for Use of Federal Funds," *Library Journal* (Series of reports under "The News" section throughout 1957. February 15: 514-515; March 15: 718-719; April 15: 1032-1035; May 15: 1292-1294; June 15: 1632-1635; July 15: 1738-1741; August: 1858-1860; September 15: 2104-2105; October 15: 2505-2508; November 15: 2898-2901; December 15: 3178-3182).

Brown, Karl. "What's Happening under LSA?" *Library Journal* 84 (February 1, 1959): 373-378.

Carlson, W. H. "Library Services Act," *Canadian Library Association Bulletin* 16 (March 1960): 228-231.

Chadwick, Catherine S. " 'Blessed Be Nothing'—To Start With," *Wilson Library Bulletin* 33 (May 1959): 642-644.

Currier, Lura Gibbon. "Forty-eight Trunk Lines NEA/ALA," *ALA Bulletin* 51 (April 1957): 285.

Cutler, Dorothy. "A Regional Library Demonstration," *Wilson Library Bulletin* 33 (May 1959): 655-658.

Dalton, Phyllis I. "The Meaning of the Library Services Act to Public Library Service," *News Notes of California Libraries* 53 (April 1958): 240-244.

Dunbar, Ralph M., and Lorenz, John G. "Uncle Sam Befriends the Library," *Saturday Review* 40 (June 22, 1957): 13-15.

Durisch, L. L. "Relationship of Local, State, and Federal Participation in Public Library Development," *Library Trends* 9 (July 1960): 105-112.

Eastlick, John T. "The Sixties and After; Special Report for Federal Relations Committee of Library Administration Division. American Library Association, 1960." Reprinted in part in *ALA Bulletin* 55 (June 1961): 556-558.

Ebert, Eloise. "The New State Grant Program," *Wilson Library Bulletin* 33 (May 1959): 659-660.

"Editorial," *ALA Bulletin* 51 (July-August 1957): 486.

Elliott, Carl. "Carl Elliott," *Wilson Library Bulletin* 34 (April 1960): 568 +.

Exton, Elaine. "Library Needs Catch Capital Spotlight," *American School Board Journal* 133 (July 1956): 45-46 +.

"54 Senators in 37 States Support LSA," *Library Journal* 85 (February 15, 1960): 732-733.

Fischer, G. J. "Library Services Bills; A Survey of Federal Aid Legislation in Congress, 1946-1955." Unpublished Master's Thesis, Case Western Reserve, 1955.

French, Zelia J. "Imagination, Manpower, and Opportunity: Strengthening a State Library Agency," *Wilson Library Bulletin* 33 (May 1959): 645-647.

Fyan, Loleta D. "Progress and Policies under the Library Services Act," *Library Quarterly* 27 (October 1957): 235-248.

Fyan, Loleta D. "You and the Library Services Act," *ALA Bulletin* 51 (January 1957): 17-19.

Goodell, C. E. "Why Extend Library Services," *ALA Bulletin* 54 (November 1960): 801-802.

Greenaway, Emerson. "Good Library Services Advanced by the Library Services Act," *Wilson Library Bulletin* 33 (May 1959): 638-641.

Greenaway, Emerson. "Rural Libraries and the Library Services Act" (Guest editorial), *Library Journal* 84 (March 15, 1959): 826.

Hamlin, Arthur T. "Library Services Act," *College and Research Libraries* 17 (September 1956): 428-429.

Harlan, Harold O. "An Urban Library Serves a County," *Wilson Library Bulletin* 33 (May 1959): 661-662.

Hill, Lister. "Libraries of the Future," *Alabama Librarian* 8 (July 1957): 49-52 + .

Hill, Lister. "Lister Hill," *Wilson Library Bulletin* 34 (April 1960): 567 + .

Hughes, M. Virginia. "Demonstrating Bookmobile Service," *Wilson Library Bulletin* 33 (May 1959): 663-666.

Javelin, Muriel C. "Adult Services under the Library Services Act," *Wilson Library Bulletin* 32 (May 1958): 637-643.

Krettek, Germaine. "Extension of the Library Services Act," *ALA Bulletin* 54 (September 1960): 653-654; (same article) *Wilson Library Bulletin* 35 (September 1960): 72.

Krettek, Germaine. "Forty Minutes," *ALA Bulletin* 54 (November 1960): 819-821.

Krettek, Germaine. "LSA, the Federal Government, and the Profession," in Strout (ed.), *Impact of the Library Services Act: Progress and Potential* (1961) pp. 17-29. See entry under Strout.

"LSA's Future Assured," (Editorial) *Library Journal* 85 (February 15, 1960): 730.

Lancour, Harold. "Summary," in Strout (ed.), *Impact of the Library Services Act: Progress and Potential* (1961) pp. 113-119. See entry under Strout.

Leigh, Carma Russell. "LSA and the Development of Library Systems," in Strout (ed.), *Impact of the Library Services Act: Progress and Potential* (1961) pp. 48-61. See entry under Strout.

"Library Services Act; Public Law 597—84th Congress, Chapter 407—2nd Session, H.R. 2840," *American Library Annual for 1956-1957*. New York: Bowker, 1958, pp. 115-117.

"Library Services Act Projects Number," (Special Issue) *Wilson Library Bulletin* 33 (May 1959).

"Library Services Act and School Libraries," *School Libraries* 6 (March 1957): 5.

"Library Services Act Resolution," *ALA Bulletin* 51 (March 1957): 211.

"Library World Shocked by Budget Cut for Library Services Act," *California Library Association News* 3 (February 1957): 1-3.

Lockhart, Elizabeth H. "Cooperative Projects Serve Children and Young Adults," *Wilson Library Bulletin* 33 (May 1959): 671-673.

Longworth, Ruth O. "A Federation of Libraries," *Wilson Library Bulletin* 33 (May 1959): 652-654.

Lorenz, John G. "Books for County People," *County Officer* 10 (October 1957): 245.

Lorenz, John G. "Getting Together and Staying Together," *Minnesota Libraries* 19 (June 1959): 115-160.

Lorenz, John G. "LSA and the Library Services Branch," in Strout (ed.), *Impact of the Library Services Act: Progress and Potential* (1961) pp. 30-39. See entry under Strout.

Lorenz, John G. "The Library Services Act," in New England Library Association. Conference, Swampscott, Mass., 1960. Addresses delivered at the New England Library Association Conference, Oct. 7, 1960, in Rhode Island Department of State. *Library Services in Rural Areas.* (1960).

Lorenz, John G. "Library Services Act—The First Three Years," *ALA Bulletin* 54 (January 1960): 17-27.

Lorenz, John G. "Library Services Branch of the U.S. Office of Education," *American Library and Book Trade Annual—1960*. New York: Bowker, 1961, pp. 69-72.

Lorenz, John G. "Library Services to the Nation (Excerpts from a Talk)," *North Carolina Libraries* 18 (Spring 1960): 83-85.

Lorenz, John G. "Progress and Projects under the Library Services Act," *Wilson Library Bulletin* 33 (May 1959): 635-637.

Lorenz, John G., and Carl, Herbert A. "The Library Services Act-A Progress Report," in *The Bowker Annual of Library and Book Trade Information, 1962*. New York: Bowker, 1961, pp. 121-127.

Lorenz, John G., and Carl, Herbert A. "Books for Rural America; Progress Report on the Library Services Act," *School Life* 40 (October 1957): 11-12.

Lorenz, John G., and Carl, Herbert A. "Library Service to Rural Areas," *Revista Interamericana de Bibliografía* 9 (October 1959): 356-361.

Lorenz, John G., and Carl, Herbert A. "The Library Services Act after Four Years," *ALA Bulletin* 55 (June 1961): 534-540.

Lorenz, John G., and Cohen, Nathan M. "More Books for Rural People," *Bookmark* 17 (May 1958): 187-191.

Luce, Helen. "Library Services Act Goes West," *ALA Bulletin* 52 (February 1958): 115-118.

Luce, Helen. "Scholarships for Rural Librarians," *Wilson Library Bulletin* 33 (May 1959): 680-681.

Luce, Helen. "Western States Library Extension Conference," *ALA Bulletin* 53 (June 1959): 526 +.

Luce, Helen, and Morin, Wilfrid L. "Five States Survey Library Needs," *ALA Bulletin* 53 (May 1959): 378-383.

McCormick, K. "Broad View of the LSA," *ALA Bulletin* 54 (May 1960): 375-377.

McDonough, Roger H. "Extension of the Library Services Act," *ALA Bulletin* 54 (March 1960): 238-239.

McDonough, Roger H. "Federal Aid to Libraries—Challenge and Opportunity," *Library Journal* 82 (September 1, 1957): 1963-1966.

McDonough, Roger H. "LSA and State Library Agencies," in Strout (ed.), *Impact of the Library Services Act: Progress and Potential* (1961) pp. 40-47. See entry under Strout.

McDonough, Roger H. "Twenty Years A-Growing: The Library Services Branch in 1958," *ALA Bulletin* 52 (January 1958): 23-27.

McGovern, George. "Statement before the Subcommittee on Labor and Health, Education, and Welfare of the House Committee on Appropriations," *South Dakota Library Bulletin* 45 (April 1959): 27.

Mahar, Mary Helen. "Implications of the Library Services Act to Children and Young People," *ALA Bulletin* 53 (February 1959): 118-122.

Martin, Lowell. "LSA and Library Standards: Two Sides of the Same Coin," in Strout (ed.), *Impact of the Library Services Act: Progress and Potential* (1961) pp. 1-16. See entry under Strout.

Martin, Lowell. "Library Standards and the Federal Program," *Library Journal* 82 (October 1, 1957): 2315-2317.

McKay, Mildred P. "A Public Information Program," *Wilson Library Bulletin* 33 (May 1959): 674-677.

Monypenny, Phillip. "LSA: A Political Scientist's View," in Strout (ed.), *Impact of the Library Services Act: Progress and Potential* (1961) pp. 93-112. See entry under Strout.

Morin, Wilfrid L. "Alaska and the Library Services Act: A Field Visit," *ALA Bulletin* 52 (September 1958): 621-624.

Morin, Wilfrid L. "Books Fly in Alaska," *Bookmark* 18 (November 1959): 29-31.

Morin, Wilfrid L. "Books for New England; Progress Report on the Library Services Act," *North Country Libraries* 1 (December 1957): 1-4.

Morin, Wilfrid L. "Interstate Library Cooperation," *Wilson Library Bulletin* 33 (May 1957): 682-685.

Morin, Wilfrid L. "The Library Services Act; A Family Project," *Illinois Libraries* 41 (February 1959): 128-134.

Morris, John D. "Budget Cutting Hits House Snag—Two Million Rise Voted Rural Libraries," *New York Times*, 30 March 1957, sec. 1, p. 12.

Mullen, Evelyn Day. "Libraries to Leeward," *School Life* 41 (January-February 1959): 11-12.

Olson, Edna. Activities of Librarians and Trustees under the Library Services Act Program; Report Prepared for American Association of Library Trustees, American Library Association Conference, San Francisco, 1958. (Mimeographed)

"Official Summary of Progress under LSA through June 1958," *Library Journal* 84 (February 15, 1959): 576-577.

Peck, Irene S. "State Regional Library Branches," *Wilson Library Bulletin* 33 (May 1959): 648-650.

Prentiss, S. Gilbert. "Research, for What?" in Strout (ed.), *Impact of the Library Services Act: Progress and Potential* (1961) pp. 79-86. See entry under Strout.

Price, Paxton P. "In-Service Training Program," *Wilson Library Bulletin* 33 (May 1959): 678-679.

Sharp, Harold S. "Cataloger's Crossword Puzzle," *Wilson Library Bulletin* 33 (May 1959): 696.

Schenk, Gretchen K. "Library Services—ABC's," *Library Journal* 82 (April 15, 1957): 1018-1023.

Smith, Hannis S. "Financing Rural Public Library Systems," in Strout (ed.), *Impact of the Library Services Act: Progress and Potential* (1961) pp. 62-78. See entry under Strout.

Strout, Donald E., ed. *Impact of the Library Services Act: Progress and Potential. Papers presented at an Institute conducted jointly by the University of Illinois Graduate School of Library Science and the Library Services Branch, U.S. Office of Education, Nov. 5-8, 1961.* (Allerton Park Institute No. 8) Champaign, Illinois: Distributed by the Illini Union Bookstore, 1962.

Sullivan, F. A. "How Is Your I.Q. on the L. S. A.?" *Library Journal* 82 (September 1957): 2162-2163.

Townsend, Silas. "Bookmobile Exhibit Project," *Wilson Library Bulletin* 33 (May 1959): 667-668.

Walker, Estellene. "Improving Reference Service," *Wilson Library Bulletin* 33 (May 1959): 669-670.

* * *

Cohen, Nathan M. *State Library Extension, Resources, and Services, 1960-61.* Washington, D.C.: U.S. Department of Health, Education, and Welfare, Office of Education, 1966.

Morin, Wilfred, and Cohen, Nathan. *State Library Extension Services; A Survey of Resources and Activities of State Library Administrative Agencies: 1955-56.* Washington, D.C.: Government Printing Office, 1960.

U.S. Congress. House. Committee on Education and Labor. *Extension of Library Services Act.* Hearings before the Subcommittee on Special Education on H.R. 9319, H.R. 9494, H.R. 9812; bills to extend the Library Services Act for a period of 5 years. 86th Congress. 2nd Session. 1960 (Held in Washington, D.C., March 29, April 6 and 7, 1960).

U.S. Congress. House. Floor Debate on the Extension of Library Services Act (S. 2830). 86th Congress. 2nd Session. August 22, 1960. *Congressional Record*, Vol. 106 Pt. 13: 17049-65.

U.S. Congress. House. Representative Fogarty speaking for increased appropriations for the Department of Labor, and Health, Education, and Welfare (H.R. 6287). 85th Congress. 1st Session. March 26, 1957. *Congressional Record*, Vol. 103:4424.

U.S. Congress. House. Subcommittee on Appropriations for the Labor Department and Health, Education, and Welfare Department. (See the *Annual Hearings and Reports Concerning Appropriations for LSA and LSCA*) 85th Congress- to date. 1957- to date.

U.S. Congress. Senate. Commmittee on Appropriations for the Labor Department and Health, Education, and Welfare Department. (See the *Annual Hearings and Reports Concerning Appropriations for LSA and LSCA*) 85th Congress- to date. 1957- to date.

U.S. Congress. Senate. Committee on Labor and Public Welfare. *Amendments to the Library Services Act.* Report to accompany S. 2830. 86th Congress. 2nd Session. 1960. Senate Report No. 1412.

U.S. Office of Education. Library Services Branch. *State Plans under the Library Services Act; A Summary of Plans and Programs for Fiscal 1957.* Prepared by the Library Services Branch. Washington, D.C.: Government Printing Office, 1958.

U.S. Office of Education. Library Services Branch. *State Plans under the Library Services Act. Supplement 1. A Summary of Programs for Fiscal 1958.* Prepared by the Library Services Branch. Washington, D.C.: Government Printing Office, 1959.

U.S. Office of Education. Library Services Branch. *State Plans under the Library Services Act. Supplement 2. A Progress Report. The First Three Years: Fiscal Years 1957, 1958, 1959.* Prepared by the

Library Services Branch. Washington, D.C.: Government Printing Office, 1960.

U.S. Office of Education. Library Services Branch. *State Plans under the Library Services Act. Supplement 3. A Progress Report. The First Five Years: Fiscal Years 1957-61.* Prepared by the Library Services Branch. Washington, D.C.: Government Printing Office, 1963.

U.S. Statutes at Large. Vol. 74. Public Law 86-679. An Act to Extend the Library Services Act for Five Years. 86th Congress. 2nd Session. August 31, 1960.

IV. Library Services Act (1961-1963)

"Amended Library Services Act," *ALA Bulletin* 56 (October 1962): 791-792.

"Amended Library Services Act for a Comprehensive Library Development Program," *ALA Washington Newsletter* 14 (May 22, 1962): 1-4.

"Comprehensive Bill to Amend Library Services Act Introduced," *Maryland Libraries* 28 (Summer 1962): 10-11+.

Comstock, Lloyd. "The Boy Who Cried Books," (Guest editorial) *Library Journal* 88 (May 15, 1963): 2087.

Connor, J. L. "New York's Accomplishments under the Federal Library Services Act, 1956-60," *Bookmark* 20 (February 1960): 91-95.

Downs, Robert B. "Library Services Act—Statements Made on H.R. 11823 before the General Subcommittee on Education of the House Committee on Education and Labor, June 27, 1962," *Illinois Libraries* 44 (November 1962): 8-9.

"Fifth Anniversary of the Library Services Act," *Publishers' Weekly* 180 (August 1961): 77.

Frantz, John C. "County and Regional Library Service; Today's Reality in America," *Minnesota Libraries* 20 (June 1962): 155-156.

French, Zelia J. *Traveling Library Story; A Report of the First Four Years under the Library Services Act.* Topeka, Kansas: Traveling Libraries Commission, 1961.

Greenaway, Emerson. "Library Needs and Federal Legislative Possibilities," *ALA Bulletin* 57 (January 1963): 31-35.

"Hearings on Amended Library Services Act," *ALA Bulletin* 56 (September 1962): 701-702.

Heckscher, A. "Libraries and the Nation's Cultural Life," *ALA Bulletin* 56 (September 1962): 716-720.

"House Debates H.R. 11823: Expanded Library Services Act," *Library Journal* 87 (September 15, 1962): 48.

Hubbard, H.W. "This May Be the Year," *Wilson Library Bulletin* 37 (September 1962): 45-48.

Krettek, Germaine. "Library Services Act and the States," *Assembly of State Librarians Proceedings, 1960*. Washington, D.C.: Library of Congress, 1961.

Krettek, Germaine. "Problems and Programs of the ALA Washington Office," *District of Columbia Libraries* 32 (April 1961): 23-26.

"Library Services Act Expanded for More Benefits," *Kansas Library Bulletin* 31 (September 1962): 26-27.

"Library Services Act Report," *Illinois Libraries* 44 (March 1962): 173-202.

Lorenz, John G. "Library Services Act and the States," *Assembly of State Librarians Proceedings, 1960*. Washington, D.C.: Library of Congress, 1961.

Lorenz, John G., and Carl, Herbert A. "Library Services Act," *ALA Bulletin* 57 (Janaury 1963): 25-26.

Lorenz, John G., and Carl, Herbert A. "Library Services Act after Four Years," *ALA Bulletin* 55 (June 1961): 534-540.

Lorenz, John G. and Carl, Herbert A. "Library Services Act—A Progress Report," *Bowker Annual of Library and Book Trade Information, 1962*. New York: Bowker, 1961, pp. 121-127.

"LSA's Fourth Year," *Wilson Library Bulletin* 35 (April 1961): 592.

Luce, Helen. "Some Results of the Library Services Act after Five Years," *Canadian Library* 19 (January 1963): 183-184.

McCarthy, E. J. "Federal Government and Rural Book Distribution," *ALA Bulletin* 57 (June 1963): 531-533.

McDonough, Roger H. "LSA—Success Story," *Library Journal* 86 (March 15, 1962): 1100-1102.

Miller, H. M. "Library Services Act in Idaho Together with a History of Public Library Development since 1901," *Idaho Librarian* 14 (July 1961): 63-73.

Moore, E. S. "Library Services Act and Public Library Development in Arizona." Unpublished Paper. Los Angeles University of Southern California, 1960.

Rohlf, Robert H. "Statement on the Revision of L.S.A.," *Minnesota Libraries* 20 (June 1963): 291-293.

U. S. Office of Education. Library Services Branch. "Library Services Act: A Five Year Progress Report," *Bowker Annual of Library and Book Trade Information, 1963*. New York: Bowker, 1963, pp. 132-143.

Vainstein, Rose. "Federal Aid to Public Library," *Canadian Library* 19 (January 1963): 211-213.

Young, Mrs. R. A. "Library Services Act: The Trustee's Role in Federal Aid," *Canadian Library* 17 (March 1961): 221-223.

* * *

Nixon, L. A. "Books for Farm People," (About Nebraska) in U.S. Department of Agriculture. *Yearbook of Agriculture,* 1962. Washington, D.C.: Government Printing Office, 1962.

U.S. Congress. House. Committee on Education and Labor. *Library Services Act; Hearings before the General Subcommittee on Education on H.R. 11823 and Similar Bills to Amend the Library Services Act.* 87th Congress. 2nd Session. 1962 (Hearings held in Washington, D.C., June 26, 27, and 29, 1962).

U.S. Congress. House. Committee on Education and Labor. *Library Services Act; Hearings before the Select Subcommittee on Education on H.R. 4879 and Similar Bills to Amend the Library Services Act to Increase the Federal Assistance for the Improvement of Public Libraries.* 88th Congress. 1st Session. 1963. (Hearings held in Washington, D.C., April 9 and 10, 1963).

U.S. Congress. Senate. Floor Debate on Amendment of Library Services Act, S. 2265. (Adjourned because of President Kennedy's assassination). 88th Congress. 1st Session. November 22, 1963. *Congressional Record,* Vol. 109. Pt. 17: 22685-92.

U.S. Congress. Senate. Resumption of Floor Debate on the Amendment of the Library Services Act, S. 2265. 88th Congress. 1st Session. November 26, 1963. *Congressional Record,* Vol. 109, Pt. 17: 22700-13.

U. S. Office of Education. Library Services Branch. *Library Services Act after Five Years.* Washington, D.C.: Government Printing Office, 1962.

U.S. President. *Public Papers of the President. John F. Kennedy.* "Special Education Message Delivered to Congress-January 29, 1963." Washington, D.C.: Government Printing Office, 1964.

U.S. Statutes at Large. Vol. 78. Public Law 87-688. (Added American Samoa to Act). 87th Congress. 2nd Session.

V.   Library Services and Construction Act (1964-1975)

Abrash, B., and Milton, J. "LSCA: Issues and Forces," in Bundy, Mary Lee and Aronson, R. (eds.). *Social and Political Aspects of Librarianship.* Albany, N.Y.: School of Library Science, State University of New York, 1965, pp. 13-22.

"Aid to Public Libraries: LSCA," *American Education* 3 (June 1967): 30-31.

Alternatives for Financing the Public Library. Prepared for the National Commission on Libraries and Information Science. Philadelphia: Government Studies and Systems, 1974.

American Library Association. Committee on Legislation. "Minutes." (Unpublished) 1960- to date.

American Library Association. Committee on Legislation. *Proceedings of the Legislative Workshop.* Washington D.C., January 28-30, 1965.

Bentley, Orville G. "The Federal Government as a Partner, " in Ladley (ed.), *Federal Legislation for Libraries* (1967) pp. 1-6. See entry under Ladley.

Berry, John N. "Amend LSCA Now," *Library Journal* 100 (March 1, 1975): 425.

Berry, John N. "Comment," (letters) *Library Journal* 100 (June 1, 1975): 790.

Black, Donald, Seiden, H. R., and, Luke, Ann W. *Evaluation of LSCA Services to Special Target Groups: Final Report.* Santa Monica, Calif.: System Development Corporation, July 1973.

Bomar, Clara P. "Federal Legislation and Interlibrary Cooperation," *Texas Library Journal* 43 (Spring 1967): 23-26.

Branscomb, Lewis C, Jr. "Let's Do It Together: The LSCA Title III Program in Ohio," *Ohio Library Association Bulletin* 41 (January 1971): 4-7.

Brinkman, G. "Correctional Libraries and LSCA Title IV-A," *American Libraries* 1 (April 1970): 380-383.

Casey, Genevieve M. (Issue editor) "Federal Aid to Libraries: Its History, Impact, and Future," *Library Trends* 24 (July 1975).

Connor, J. L. "Stages in and the Fields for Interlibrary Cooperation," *Bookmark* 27 (October 1967): 13-18.

Cooke, Eileen. "Libraries and General Revenue Sharing: Charts Compare Dollar Amounts for Libraries Within Each State under Revenue Sharing in 1972 and 1973, with LSCA Dollar Amounts for Each State in Fiscal Year 1972," *American Libraries* 4 (July 1973): 434-436.

Cooke, Eileen. "Library Outlook from Capitol Hill," *New Mexico Library Bulletin* 36 (Spring 1967): 414-422.

Cooke, Eileen, and Case, Sara. "Appropriations and Impoundment," *American Libraries* 4 (November 1973): 631.

Cooke, Eileen, and Case, Sara. "Independent Research Libraries," *Wilson Library Bulletin* 48 (November 1973): 216.

Cooke, Eileen, and Case, Sara. "New LSCA Title Vetoed," *American Libraries* 4 (January 1973): 36.

Courtright, H. R. "State Library Agency Directors Conference on Implementation of Public Law 91-600," Association of State Library Agencies *President's Newsletter* 1 (Summer 1971): 7-9.

Crowe, Linda, et al. "If They Could Solve the (Library) Problems in Champaign-Urbana, They'd Have the Solutions to the World's Problems: A Field Report," *Wilson Library Bulletin* 47 (November 1972): 283-289.

Currier, Lura G. "Defense Never Rests; Testifying for the Library Services and Contruction Act Before the House Select Education Subcommittee on Education," *ALA Bulletin* 60 (July 1966): 705-710.

Currier, Lura G. "Excerpts and Comment, Entitled: We Have With Us Today as a Witness," *Mississippi Library News* 30 (September 1966): 89-93.

Davison, R. M. "Library Services Act in Indiana, 1955-1963." *ACRL Microcard Series No. 143.* Chicago: Association of College and Research Libraries, 1964. (Same as Unpublished Master's Thesis, University of Indiana, 1964.)

"FY '74: Token LSCA, ESEA funds," *Wilson Library Bulletin* 48 (October 1973): 136-137.

"Federal Fund Cuts Seen Catastropic; State Librarians Polled by LJ Tally Drastic Cuts Seen in Staff and Services," *Library Journal* 94 (May 15, 1969): 1929-1930+.

"Fiscal 1965 LSCA Programs Spend Record $130 Million," *Library Journal* 91 (April 15, 1966): 2021-2022.

Fogarty, John. "Laws, Law-Makers, and Libraries," in *Proceedings of the Legislative Workshop.* American Library Association, Committee on Legislation, Washington, D.C., January 28-30, 1965.

Fox, June T. "Library Planning and Evaluation Institute: Helping State Libraries Write Effective Long-Term Programs," *American Libraries* 3 (May 1972): 501-505.

Frantz, John C. "Library Services Act—Library Services and Construction Act," *Illinois Libraries* 47 (January 1965): 3-12.

Frantz, John C. "Library Services and Construction Act," *ALA Bulletin* 60 (February 1966):149-152.

Frantz, John C., and Cohen, Nathan M. "The Federal Government and Public Libraries: A Ten-Year Partnership, 1957-1966." Reprint. Springfield, Illinois: Illinois State Library, no date.

Frase, Robert W. *Library Funding and Public Support.* Chicago: American Library Association, 1973.

Frase, Robert W. "Five Years of Struggle for Federal Funds," *Publishers Weekly* 205 (January 21, 1974): 64-67.

Fry, James W. "LSA and LSCA, 1956-1973: A Legislative History," *Library Trends* 24 (July 1975): 7-26.

Fry, Ray McNair. "New Team at the Top," *Library Journal* 93 (January 1, 1968): 43-48.

Gesterfield, Kathryn. "Challenge and Hope: The Library Services and Construction Act," *Illinois Libraries* 53 (April-May 1971): 315-326.

Glazer, Frederic J., and Haynes, Donald R. "Observations on the Persecution and Assassination of LSCA as Performed by the Inmates of the Office of Education under the Direction of Peter Muirhead," *Library Journal* 98 (June 15, 1973): 887-889.

"Guidelines for Preparing a Proposal for a Library Services and Construction Act Grant (Titles I, II, III)," *Illinois Libraries* 55 (November 1973): 750-767; 57 (October 1975): 580-596.

"HEW Appropriations Passes; LSCA to Get $55 Million," *Library Journal* 90 (September 15, 1965): 3570.

Hannigan, Margaret C. "From Darkness into Light," *Association of Hospital and Institutional Libraries Quarterly* 10 (Summer 1970): 46-48.

Hannigan, Margaret C. "Has the Public Law 89-522 Affected Your Library?" *Assocation of Hospital and Institutional Libraries Quarterly* 9 (Fall 1968): 4-5.

Hannigan, Margaret C. "Library Services to the Physically Handicapped in Maine, Texas, and Delaware," *Association of Hospital and Institutional Libraries Quarterly* 10 (Fall 1969): 16-17.

Hannigan, Margaret C. "On the Plus Side, Institutional Library Development Since 1966," *Association of Hospital and Institutional Libraries Quarterly* 9 (Spring 1969): 63-65.

Hannigan, Margaret C. "Our New Perspective," *Association of Hospital and Institutional Libraries Quarterly* 9 (Summer 1968): 93.

Hannigan, Margaret C. "Training for Library Service to the Institutionalized and Handicapped; Short-Term Institutes on Library Services to the Institutionalized, the Handicapped, the Aging and Exceptional Children," *Association of Hospital and Institutional Libraries Quarterly* 11 (Fall 1970): 7-8.

Hansell, J. "Indiana Libraries Progress with LSCA, 1961-67," *Library Occurrent* 22 (February 1967): 106-112.

Hope, A. "When I Was Five: Half a Decade of LSCA in New England," *Library Journal* 94 (October 15, 1969): 3622-3625.

"House Appropriations Committee Omits Provision for LSCA Funds," *Library Journal* 89 (May 15, 1964): 2048.

"House Approves Expanded Library Services Act," *Publishers' Weekly* 185 (February 3, 1964): 65.

"House Passes Appropriations Bill Including $55 Million for LSCA," *Library Journal* 90 (June 1, 1965): 2512.

"House Passes H.R. 4879 after Four-Hour Debate," *Library Journal* 89 (February 15, 1964): 824.

Hughey, Elizabeth H. "Library Services and Construction Act, as Amended," *Bowker Annual of Library and Book Trade Information, 1969-75*. New York: Bowker, 1969-75.

Igoe, James G. "Federal Grants and Public Libraries," *Advances in Librarianship*, vol. 3. New York: Seminar Press, 1972, pp. 137-165.

Igoe, James G. "New in the Old Northwest: A Quick Survey of Library Activity in USOE's Region V," *Library Journal* 94 (November 1969): 4112-4115.

Javits, Jacob, et al. "LSCA Amendments of 1966," (Excerpts from February 18, 1966, *Congressional Record*—Senate) *Bookmark* 25 (April 1966): 253-256.

Kee, S. Janice. "Cooperation Moves Ahead in the Southwest; A Report on the Progress to Date Achieved under the Library Services and Construction Act," *Library Journal* 95 (April 1, 1970): 1294-1297.

Kee, S. Janice. "The Impact of Federal Legislation on Public Libraries," in Ladley (ed.), *Federal Legislation for Libraries* (1967) pp. 7-21. See entry under Ladley.

Kee, S. Janice. "Library Planning: Trends and Programs in the Southwest," *New Mexico Libraries* 2 (Summer 1969): 33-41.

Kittel, Dorothy A. "Trends in State Library Cooperation," *Library Trends* 24 (October 1975): 245-255.

Knight, Douglas M., and Nourse, E. Shepley (comps.) *Libraries at Large; Tradition, Innovation, and the National Interest. The Resource Book Based on the Materials of the National Advisory Commission on Libraries*. New York: Bowker, 1969.

Krettek, Germaine. "Building Legislative Support for Library Programs: 1957-1972," *American Libraries* 4 (January 1973): 42-44.

Krettek, Germaine. "Library Legislation, Federal," in *Encyclopedia of Library and Information Science*, vol. 15. New York: Marcel Dekker, 1975, pp. 337-354.

Krettek, Germaine, and Cooke, Eileen. "Expanded LSCA Signed by President," *Wilson Library Bulletin* 41 (September 1966): 102-103.

Krettek, Germaine, and Cooke, Eileen. "LSCA Signed as Congress Adjourns," *American Libraries* 2 (February 1971): 175-176.

Ladley, Winifred (ed.). *Federal Legislation for Libraries. Papers Presented at an Institute Conducted by the University of Illinois Graduate School of Library Science, November 6-9, 1966*. (Allerton Park Institute Champaign, Illinois: Distributed by the Illini Union Bookstore, 1967. No. 13).

Lane, Rodney. *Basic Issues in the Governmental Financing of Public Library Services.* A Commissioned Paper under the Commissioned Papers Project, Teachers College, Columbia University. Philadelphia: Government Studies and Systems, 1973.

Leigh, Carma. "The Role of the American Library Association in Federal Legislation for Libraries," in Ladley (ed.), *Federal Legislation for Libraries* (1967) pp. 76-88. See entry under Ladley.

Lorenz, John G. "Uncle Sam and Public Libraries," in Virginia Young, ed., *The Library Trustee; A Practical Guide.* New York: Bowker, 1964, pp. 131-147.

Low, Edmon. "Federal Consciousness and Libraries," *American Libraries* 3 (July/August 1972): 717-721.

"LSCA Extended Through FY 1976," *Wilson Library Bulletin* 45 (February 1971): 607.

"LSCA Funds Stalled by Ford Tactics," *American Libraries* 6 (September 1975): 470-471.

"LSCA in Arkansas,"
"LSCA in California,"
"LSCA in Kansas,"
"LSCA in Massachusetts,"
"LSCA in New York,"
"LSCA in North Carolina,"
"LSCA in Ohio,"
"LSCA in South Carolina,"
"LSCA in Utah,"
"LSCA in Washington,"
"LSCA in Wisconsin,"
(State-by-State summaries in System Development Corporation, Santa Monica, Calif. *Overview of the Library Services and Construction Act, Title I.* New York: Bowker, 1969. See entry under System Development Corporation.)

"LSCA Amendments Voted by Congress: House, 336-2; Senate, Unanimous," *Library Journal* 91 (July 1966): 3368.

"LSCA and Higher Education Grants Total $110 Million for Construction," *Library Journal* 90 (July 1965): 2986+.

"LSCA Appropriation Signed by President Johnson," *Library Journal* 89 (October 1, 1964): 3708.

"LSCA-1968 Down 50 Percent from Total Authorization," *Library Journal* 92 (July 1967): 2494.

"LSCA Public Library Construction, 1965," *ALA Bulletin* 61 (January 1965): 28-29.

"LSCA; Ten-Year Summary and Evaluation, New Mexico, 1956-1966," *New Mexico Libraries* 35 (Fall 1966): 369-371.

"Library Services and Construction Act: Amendments of 1970 as Amended Through August 21, 1974," (text) *Illinois Libraries* 57 (October 1975): 597-617.

"Library Services and Construction Act: What It Can and Can't Do," *Kansas Library Bulletin* 41 (No. 2, 1972): 22-23.

"Library Services and Construction Act Approved by the Senate in 89-7 Vote," *Library Journal* 89 (January 15, 1964): 335-336.

"Library Services and Construction Act; Background and Text," *School Life* 46 (May 1964): 23-26.

"Library Services and Construction Amendments of 1970," (text) *Texas Libraries* 33 (Fall 1971): 121-131. Also in *Illinois Libraries* 54 (November 1972): 802-809; 55 (November 1973): 658-665.

McClarren, Robert R. "Federal Financial Assistance," in Alphonse F. Trezza, ed., *Proceedings of the Library Buildings Institute, 1967.* Chicago: American Library Association, 1972, pp. 135-141.

McCrossan, John A. "Interlibrary Cooperation," *Pennsylvania Library Association* 26 (May 1971): 167-169.

McCrossan, John A. "Middle Atlantic State Library Agencies Discuss Interlibrary Cooperation," Association of State Library Agencies *President's Newsletter* 1 (Summer 1971): 1-3.

Madden, Dorothea R. "Thinking Out Loud," in E. J. Josey, ed., *What Black Librarians Are Saying.* Metuchen, N.J.: Scarecrow Press, 1972, pp. 227-230.

Martin, Lowell. "Library Development under the Library Services Act and Library Services and Construction Act; An Informal Report to the U.S. Commissioner of Education," (Typescript) 1966.

Martin, Lowell. "Library Services and Construction Act--What Will It Mean?" *ALA Bulletin* 58 (September 1964): 689-694.

"Massachusetts Congressmen Endorse Library Law," *Bay State Librarian* 54 (Janaury 1964): 15.

Nelson, W. D. "Library Funds Vetoed by Ford," *Wilson Library Bulletin* 50 (September 1975): 15.

Olson, E. B. "Library Services and Construction Act of 1964 and the Amendments of 1966: A Legislative Case Study." Unpublished Master's Thesis, University of Texas, 1967.

Potter, V. E. "That Special Project You Tucked Away: LSCA Funds for Public Library Services," *Wisconsin Library Bulletin* 68 (November 1972): 419-420.

"President Signs LSCA Amendments of 1966; Announces National Library Commission," *Library Journal* 91 (August 1966): 3666.

"President Signs $135 Million Library Bill," *Library Journal* 89 (March 1, 1964): 1046-1047.

Price, Paxton P. "LSCA, Opportunity Unlimited," *North Country Libraries* 7 (July 1964): 1-4.

Price, Paxton P. "LSCA, the Official View," *ALA Bulletin* 58 (September 1964): 694-696.

"Programs and Progress under Title IV-B (Library Services to the Physically Handicapped) Maine, Vermont, and New Hampshire," *North Country Libraries* 11 (March 1968): 47-49.

Reynolds, Maryann E. "LSA, 1956-64, LSCA, 1964," *Washington State Library News Bulletin* 31 (July 1965): 173-181.

"Role and Limitations of the LSCA Program in Library Development," *Texas Libraries* 30 (Fall 1968): 88-91.

Rosenfeld, H. E. "Urban Libraries Council: Over to You, ALA," *Wilson Library Bulletin* 49 (March 1975):482.

Rowell, J. A. "Title III: Yet Once More," *Library Journal* 92 (October 15, 1967): 3823 +.

"Senate Votes Funds for LSCA; Bill Now Goes to Conference," *Library Journal* 89 (September 15, 1964): 3276.

Shubert, Joseph F. "Impact of the Federal Library Services and Construction Act," *Library Trends* 24 (July 1975): 27-44.

"Signing of PL 88-269," *Catholic Library World* 36 (September 1964):15.

"State librarians Meet in Washington to Discuss Termination of LSCA," Association of State Library Agencies *President's Newsletter* 3 (Spring 1973): 2-3.

Stephens, Denny R. "Library Services and Construction Act," *Kansas Library Bulletin* 40, No. 1 (1970): 20-23.

"Study of LSCA Title I Heaps Praise on States," *Library Journal* 94 (May 1, 1969): 1826.

"Summary of State Library Services Act and Library Services and Construction Act Program in Ten-Year Period Ending June 30, 1966," *News Notes of California Libraries* 62 (Summer 1967): 337-342.

Swank, Raynard C. "Interlibrary Cooperation under Title III of the Library Services and Construction Act; A Preliminary Study for the California State Library. Sacramento, California: State Library, 1967. Summary by V. L. Ross. *News Notes of California Libraries* 65: Supplement (Winter 1970): 367-375.

System Development Corporation (Santa Monica, Calif.) *An Overview of the Library Services and Construction Act—Title I.* Edited by Jules Mersel, et al. New York: Bowker, 1969.

"Ten Years of Public Library Development in Iowa, under LSA and LSCA (1956-1966)," *Iowa Library Quarterly* 20 (October 1966): 149-162.

"Ten Years of the LSA-LSCA in Minnesota," *Minnesota Libraries* 21 (September 1966): 332-335.

"ULC $$ Proposal Is the Focus of D.C. Meeting," *Library Journal* 100 (August 1975): 1374-1375.

U. S. Office of Education. "The Library Services Act: A Five-Year Progress Report," *Bowker Annual of Library and Book Trade Information, 1963.* New York: Bowker, 1963.

U. S. Office of Education. "Library Services, Public Library Construction, and Interlibrary Cooperation: Procedures for Financial Assistance under the Library Services and Construction Act, as Amended," *Illinois Libraries* 55 (November 1973): 665-680.

U. S. Office of Education. "Library Services, Public Library Construction, and Interlibrary Cooperation: Proposed Procedures for Financial Assistance under the Library Services and Construction Act, as Amended," *Texas Libraries* 33 (Fall 1971): 132-154. Also in *Illinois Libraries* 54 (November 1972): 809-823.

U. S. Office of Education. Library Services Branch. "LSCA; Legislation into Action," *Library Journal* 89 (September 1, 1964): 3099-3103.

U. S. Office of Education. Library Services Branch (compilers). "Library Services and Construction Act: Regulations Applicable to the Administration of the Library Services and Construction Act," *Illinois Libraries* 48 (January 1966): 961-983.

U. S. Office of Education. Library Services Branch (compilers). "Library Services and Construction Act: Regulations Applicable to the Administration of the Library Services and Construction Act," *Illinois Libraries* 50 (January 1968): 78-108.

U. S. Office of Education. Library Services Branch. "Library Services Act—Progress Report," *Bowker Annual of Library and Book Trade Information, 1964.* New York: Bowker, 1964.

Vale, M. R. "Regionalization Has Nine Lives," *Library Journal* 94 (September 15, 1969): 3016-3018.

Wang, R. "Please Don't Shut the Door! The Library Services and Construction Act (LSCA)," *Association of Hospital and Institutional Libraries Quarterly* 13 (Summer-Fall 1973): 29-32.

"Washington Trip Pays Off," *New York Library Association Bulletin* 23 (May 1975): 7.

"Yearlong Training Program Dominates 1971-72 for State Librarians and Planners," Association of State Library Agencies *President's Newsletter* 2 (Spring 1972): 3-4.

* * *

Erteschik, Ann M., Buchko, Jr., Michael, and Hirsch, Julia M. (compilers) *Public Library Construction, 1965-1978: The Federal Con-*

tribution Through the Library Services and Construction Act. Washington, D.C.: U. S. Office of Education, 1978.

Frantz, John C., and Cohen, Nathan M. *The Federal Government and Public Libraries: A Ten-Year Partnership, 1957-1966.* Reprint from *Health, Education, and Welfare Indicators,* July 1966.

Kittel, Dorothy A. *Trends in State Library Cooperation.* Washington, D.C.: U. S. Office of Education, 1975.

Price, Paxton P. "Public Library Program Amendments of 1966 (P.L. 89-511)." Reprint from *Health, Education, and Welfare Indicators,* September 1966.

U.S. Comptroller General. *Federal Library Support Programs: Progress and Problems.* Report to the Congress. Washington, D.C.: General Accounting Office, 1974.

U.S. Congress. House. Committee on Education and Labor. *Library Services and Construction Act Amendments, 1966. Hearings before the Select Subcommittee on Education on H.R. 14050, a Bill to Extend and Amend the Library Services and Construction Act.* 89th Congress, 2nd Session. 1966 (Held in Washington, D.C., April 19, 20, 21, and 25, 1966).

U. S. Congress. Senate. Committee on Labor and Public Welfare. Committee Print, *The Library Services and Construction Act of 1964: A Compilation of Material Relevant to Public Law 88-269.* 88th Congress. 2nd Session. 1964.

U. S. Congress. Senate. Committee on Labor and Public Welfare. *Library Services and Construction Act Amendments. Hearing on S. 2802, S. 2944, and S. 3076; Bills to Amend the Library Services and Construction Act.* 89th Congress. 2nd Session. 1966 (Held in Washington, D.C., May 20, 1966).

U.S. Congress. House. Committee on Education and Labor. *To Amend the Library Services and Construction Act. Hearings before the Select Subcommittee on Education on H.R. 9518 and H.R. 12567; Bills to Amend the Library Services and Construction Act with Respect to the Extent of the Required Matching under Titles III and IV.* 90th Congress. 1st Session. 1967 (Hearing held in Washington, D.C., August 30, 1967).

U.S. Congress. Senate. Committee on Labor and Public Welfare. *Library Services and Construction Amendments of 1970. Hearing before the Subcommittee on Education on S. 3318; To Amend the Library Services and Construction Act, and for Other Purposes.* 91st Congress. 2nd Session. 1970 (Hearing held in Washington, D.C., January 27, 1970).

U.S. Congress. House. Committee on Education and Labor. *Library Services and Construction Amendments of 1970. Hearing before the Select Subcommittee on Education on H.R. 16365 and S. 3318; Bills to Extend, Consolidate and Improve Programs under the Library Services and Construction Act.* 91st Congress. 2nd Session. 1970 (Hearing held in Washington, D.C., September 10, 1970).

U.S. Congress. House. Committee on Education and Labor. *Library Services Extension. Hearing before the Subcommittee on Select Education on H.R. 11233 to Amend the Library Services and Construction Act to Extend the Authorizations of Appropriations Contained in Such Act, and for Other Purposes; and H.R. 10999 to Authorize the Secretary of Health, Education, and Welfare to Distribute Funds to Recording for the Blind, Incorporated, to Assist Such Corporation in Carrying Out Certain Projects.* 94th Congress. 1st Session. 1976 (Hearing held in Washington, D.C., December 15, 1975).

U.S. President. *Public Papers of the President. Lyndon B. Johnson.* "Annual Message to the Congress on the State of the Union-January 8, 1964." Washington, D.C.: Government Printing Office, 1965, pp. 112-118.

U.S. Statutes at Large. Vol. 78. Public Law 88-269. "Library Services and Construction Act." (Amended the Library Services Act to Include Urban Areas and Title II, Construction, and Extended the Program to the District of Columbia). 88th Congress. 2nd Session. February 11, 1964.

U.S. Statutes at Large. Vol. 80. Public Law 89-511. "Library Services and Construction Act Amendments of 1966." (Extension of Act for Five Years, Added Title III, Interlibrary Cooperation, Title IV A, Institutions, and Title IV B, Physically Handicapped, and Included Trust Territory of the Pacific Islands). 89th Congress. 2nd Session. July 19, 1966.

U.S. Statutes at Large. Vol. 81. Public Law 90-154. "Library Services and Construction Act Amendments of 1967." (Technical Amendments to Permit Acquisition of Existing Buildings for Public Library Use under Title II). 90th Congress. 1st Session. November 24, 1967.

U.S. Statutes at Large. Vol. 84, pt. 2. Public Law 1-600. "Library Services and Construction Act Amendments of 1970." (Extension of Act for Five Years; Consolidates Titles I, IV-A, and IV-B; Emphasizes Services to Low-Income Families, Strengthening State Library Agencies, and Metropolitan Libraries Which Serve as National or Regional Resource Centers; Removes Matching Requirements for Interlibrary Cooperation, Title III; and Streamlines State Plan Procedures). 91st Congress. 2nd Session. December 30, 1970.

U.S. Statutes at Large. Vol. 87. Public Law 93-73. "Older Americans Comprehensive Services Amendments of 1973 to Add Title IV, 'Older Readers Services,' to the Library Services and Construction Act." (This title never funded). 93rd Congress. 1st Session. May 3, 1973.

U.S. Statutes at Large. Vol. 87. Public Law 93-133. "National Foundation on the Arts and the Humanities Amendments of 1973." (Amendment to the Library Services and Construction Act to Enlarge the Definition of 'Public Libraries' to Include Research Libraries Meeting Specific Criteria). 93rd Congress. 1st Session. November 19, 1973.

U.S. Statutes at Large. Vol. 88. Public Law 93-380. "Educational Amendments of 1974." (Amendment to Library Services and Construction Act to Add Program Priority for Service to High Concentrations of Persons with Limited English-Speaking Ability). 93rd Congress. 2nd Session. July 21, 1974.

VI. Library Services and Construction Act (1976-1981)

American Library Association. *Legislative Report of the ALA Washington Office.* (Issued Semi-annually at Midwinter and Annual ALA Conferences.)

"Another Ford Veto, Another Override," *School Library Journal* 23 (November 1976): 12.

"Battle of '76: LSCA Extension Now on the Fight Card in House Arena; In This Corner: ALA, ULC, NCLIS, et al; Opposite Corner: Administration, U.S.O.E.," *American Libraries* 7 (February 1976): 76.

"Big Urban Libraries Lack LSCA Trigger Priority," *Library Journal* 104 (July 1979): 1407.

Boorstin, Glazer, et al. "Dramatize Importance of LSCA at House Hearings," *American Libraries* 12 (November 1981): 596-597.

Brademas, John. "The Future of Federal Library Support," *Library Journal* (January 1, 1976): 35-37.

"Brademas Compromise Wins LSCA Extension," *American Libraries* 8 (October 1977): 469.

"Carter Signs LSCA Extension," *American Libraries* 8 (November 1977): 531.

Case, Sara. "Library Services and Construction Act," *Special Libraries* 67 (March 1976): 169.

Casey, Genevieve M. "Administration of State and Federal Funds for Library Development," *Library Trends* 27 (Fall 1978): 145-163.

Cohn, John M. "Federal Aid and Local Spending: Stimulation vs. Substitution," *Library Journal* 104 (February 15, 1979): 457-459.

"Congress Reauthorizes LSCA at Lower Funding Levels," *Library Journal* 106 (October 15, 1981): 1928.

"Congress Begins Hearings on Library Services Act," *American Libraries* 8 (March 1977): 110+.

Cooke, Eileen D., and Henderson, Carol C. "House Approves LSCA Extension," *Wilson Library Bulletin* 50 (April 1976): 654.

Cooke, Eileen D., and Henderson, Carol C. "LSCA Extension Bills Introduced in the House," *Wilson Library Bulletin* 51 (February 1976): 471+.

Cooke, Eileen D., and Henderson, Carol C. "LSCA Extension Bill Pending," *Wilson Library Bulletin* 51 (April 1977): 670.

Cooke, Eileen D., and Henderson, Carol C. "LSCA Extension Developments," *Wilson Library Bulletin* 51 (June 1976): 861.

Cooke, Eileen D., and Henderson, Carol C. "LSCA Extension to House Floor," *Wilson Library Bulletin* 50 (March 1976): 558-559.

Cooke, Eileen D,. and Sprouse, H. W. "LSCA Signed into Law," *Wilson Library Bulletin* 52 (November 1977): 252.

"COSLA Urges More LSCA $$ for State Library Agencies," *Library Journal* 102 (January 15, 1977): 149.

"Deadline Nears for LSCA Extension Act," *American Libraries* 8 (September 1977): 406-407.

"Direct Aid for City Libraries Endorsed by ALA," *Library Journal* 101 (September 1, 1976): 1682.

Drennan, Henry T. "Institutional Libraries: Federal Perspectives," *Library Trends* 26 (Winter 1978): 341-360.

Drennan, Henry T. "Legislative Bases of Federal Support for Public Library and Information Services to the Handicapped," *Information: Reports and Bibliographies* (New York: Science Assocates International) 7, No. 2 (1978): 38-40.

"Federal Aid to Libraries: HEA & LSCA Prospects," *Library Journal* 101 (February 1976): 465-466.

Ford, W. D. "Federal Library Programs: Past, Present, and Future," *Library Journal* 104 (September 15, 1979): 1768-1772.

Gell, Marilyn K. "Legislative Two-Step (LSCA)," *Library Journal* 106 (October 15, 1981): 1969.

Gregory, Ruth W. (compiler). "Federal Funds and Library Development in Illinois," (Special Issue) *Illinois Libraries* 62 (June 1980).

"Guidelines for Preparing a Proposal for a Library Services and Construction Act Grant," *Illinois Libraries* 58 (October 1976): 634-650; 59 (November 1977): 713-729; 61 (May 1979): 461-477; 62 (May 1980): 461-478.

"HEW Approves Portable Libraries," *Wilson Library Bulletin* 53 (June 1979): 684.

Hansell, J. "Indiana Libraries Progress with LSCA," *Libraries Occurrent* 25 (May 1976): 215-233.

"House Closes LSCA Funds Gap," *American Libraries* 7 (June 1976): 315.

"House Group Approves LSCA Extension Bill," *American Libraries* 7 (March 1976): 122.

Hughey, Elizabeth. "Library Services and Construction Act," *Bowker Annual of Library and Book Trade Information*. 20th-25th Editions. New York: Bowker, 1975-80.

"LSCA in California," (Special Issue) *News Notes of California Libraries* 71, No. 2 (1976).

Ladenson, Alex. "Overhauling the Library Services and Construction Act," *Library Journal* 103 (May 15, 1978): 1025-1029.

Ladoff, N. S. "On Federal Aid (Statement for the Joint Oversight Hearings on Federal Library Programs)," *Public Libraries* 18 (Fall 1979): 55-56.

Leigh, Carma. "Remembrances on the Occasion of LSCA's 25th Anniversary," *ALA Yearbook, 1982*. Chicago: American Library Association, 1982, pp. 284-285.

"Library Community Rallies Against LSCA Threat," *Library Journal* 101 (February 15, 1976): 568.

"Library Services and Construction Act," in *Bowker Annual of Library and Book Trade Information, 1981*. New York: Bowker, 1981, pp. 162-172.

"Library Services and Construction Act; Amendments of 1970 as Amended through August, 1974," *Illinois Libraries* 58 (October 1976): 651-671.

"Library Services and Construction Act; Amendments of 1970 as Amended through October 7, 1977," *Illinois Libraries* 59 (November 1977): 730-752. Also, 61 (May 1979): 478-500; 62 (May 1980): 479-501.

Molz, Redmond Kathleen. *Federal Policy and Library Support*. Cambridge, Mass.: MIT Press, 1976.

"NCLIS Calls for LSCA Revision: More $$, More Safeguards," *Library Journal* 101 (February 1, 1976): 461.

"NCLIS Proposes New Pattern for Federal Funding," *Library Journal* 103 (August 1978): 1454-1455.

"N. E. State Library Coalition Opposes LSCA Cutbacks," *Library Journal* 106 (May 1, 1981): 929-930.

Nelson, W. D. "LSCA Bill Takes First Steps on the Tortuous Path to Enactment," *Wilson Library Bulletin* 50 (February 1976): 434.

Nelson, W. D. "LSCA Extended, with New Provisions for Urban Public Libraries," *Wilson Library Bulletin* 52 (November 1977): 213.

Nelson, W. D. "Senate Committee Backs Urban Library Aid," *Wilson Library Bulletin* 51 (June 1977): 213.

Nelson, W. D. "Tough Sledding for Proposed Urban LSCA Title," *Wilson Library Bulletin* 51 (April 1977): 625.

Nelson, W. D. "Urban Libraries Title Dropped from the House LSCA Bill," *Wilson Library Bulletin* 51 (May 1977): 715.

"New Educational Commissioner Backs Libraries as Schools," *American Libraries* 8 (May 1977): 233-234.

"New LSCA Title V Draft Proposed by ULC," *Library Journal* 101 (March 15, 1976): 772.

"Northeast Library Coalition Tells What LSCA Has Done," *Library Journal* 106 (October 15, 1981): 1984.

Nyren, Karl E. "Uncle Sam and the Public Library," *Library Journal* 101 (February 1976): 459.

"Opposition to Title V Voiced by Agency People," *Library Journal* 102 (May 15, 1977): 1085.

"Proposed National Library and Information Services Act to Replace LSCA," *Public Libraries* 20 (Summer 1981): 60-61.

Savage, Noel. "Co-Op Options, $$ Roles Debated at ASLA," *Library Journal* 102 (May 15, 1977): 1104. Comment by Anne Marie Falsone, (Letter) *Library Journal* 102 (October 1, 1977): 1975.

Schuchat, Theodor. "A Quarter-Century of Library Progress." (Pamphlet) Washington, D.C.: American Library Association, June 1981.

"Senate Bill Favors Urban Libraries," *American Libraries* 8 (June 1977): 287.

" '77 Library Appropriations Stalled by Abortion Fight," *American Libraries* 7 (September 1977): 491+.

Sevigny, Alan. "Emergence of the Multistate Region," in Beth Hamilton and William B. Ernst, Jr., ed. *Multitype Library Cooperation*. New York: Bowker, 1977, pp. 48-54.

Simmons, B. D. "Library Services and Construction Act," *Catholic Library World* 52 (December 1980): 232+.

"Special Urban Aid Part of LSCA Bill," *Library Journal* 102 (April 1, 1977): 754.

"State Library Agencies Face State, Federal $$ Cuts," *Library Journal* 106 (February 15, 1981): 402-403.

"Threats to State Agencies $$ Roles Shaping Up," *Library Journal* 102 (May 15, 1977): 1090+.

"Title II Grants Assist Construction of 97 Texas Public Library Buildings," *Texas Libraries* 40 (Fall 1978): 101-115.

"Urban Libraries Inch Toward Federal Aid," *American Libraries* 8 (March 1977): 112.

"Urban Libraries Heavies Come Out Smokin'," *American Libraries* 7 (March 1976): 135.

Wagner, S. "House-Senate Group Agrees on Urban Library Funding," *Publishers Weekly* 212 (October 1977): 35-36.

Winnick, Pauline. "LSCA and Service for Children," *Public Library Association Newsletter* 15 (Winter 1976): 3-5.

* * *

Casey, Joseph, Linehan, Ronald, and West, Walter. *An Evaluation of Title I of the Library Services and Construction Act. Final Report, January, 1981.* Prepared for Office of Program Evaluation, U.S. Office of Education. Washington, D.C.: Applied Management Sciences, 1981.

Casey, Joseph, Linehan, Ronald, and West, Walter. *An Evaluation of Title I of the Library Services and Construction Act. Summary Report.*Washington, D.C.: Applied Management Sciences, 1981.

Erteschik, Ann. *Library Programs Worth Knowing About.* 2nd. ed. Prepared by Ann Erteschik, State and Public Library Services Branch, Office of Libraries and Learning Technologies, for U.S. Office of Education and Chief Officers of State Library Agencies. Washington, D.C.: U.S. Office of Education, Chief Officers of State Library Agencies, 1977.

Erteschik, Ann M., Buchko, Jr., Michael, and Hirsch, Julia M., (comps.). *Public Library Construction, 1965-1978; The Federal Contribution Through the Library Services and Construction Act.* Washington, D.C.: U.S. Office of Education, 1978.

Far West Laboratory for Educational Research and Development, San Francisco, Calif. *Library Programs Worth Knowing About.* Preliminary Edition. Prepared for the U.S. Office of Education by the Far West Laboratory for Educational Research and Development. Washington, D.C.: U.S. Department of Health, Education, and Welfare (Bureau of School Systems, Office of Libraries and Learning Resources), 1976.

Lane, Rodney P. *Evaluation of the Effectiveness of Federal Funding of Public Libraries.* A Study Prepared for the National Commission on Libraries and Information Science. Washington, D.C.: Government Printing Office, 1976.

Leonard, Lawrence, and Buchko, Jr., Michael, (comps.) *Federal Programs for Libraries: A Directory.* 2nd. ed. Washington, D.C.:

U.S. Office of Education. Office of Libraries and Learning Resources, 1979.

Patrick, Ruth J., Casey, Joseph, and Novalis, Carol M. *A Study of Library Cooperatives, Networks, and Demonstration Projects.* New York: K. G. Saur, 1980.

Public Libraries: Who Should Pay the Bills? (Pamphlet written by Alice Norton for the National Commission on Libraries and Information Science.) Washington, D.C.: Government Printing Office, 1978.

U.S. Advisory Commission on Intergovernmental Relations. *Federal Involvement in Libraries.* Washington, D.C., June 1980.

U.S. Congress. House. Committee on Education and Labor. *Library Services Extension; Hearing before the Subcommittee on Select Education on H.R. 11233 to Amend the Library Services and Construction Act, to Extend the Authorizations of Appropriations Contained in Such Act, and for Other Purposes.* . . . 94th Congress. 1st Session. 1976 (Hearings held in Washington, D.C., December 15, 1975).

U.S. Congress. House. Committee on Education and Labor. *Proposed Extension of the Library Services and Construction Act; Hearing before the Subcommittee on Select Education.* 95th Congress. 1st Session. 1977 (Hearings held in Washington, D.C., February 16, 1977).

U.S. Congress. House. Committee on Education and Labor. *Library Services and Construction Act Extension.* Report to Accompany H.R. 3712. 95th Congress. 1st Session. 1977. H. Report 95-97.

U.S. Congress. House. Committee on Education and Labor. *Library Services and Construction Act Extension.* Report of Committee on Conference. 95th Congress. 1st Session. 1977. H. Report 95-607.

U.S. Congress. Senate. Committee on Human Resources. *Library Services and Construction Act Extension.* 95th Congress. 1st Session. 1977. S. Report 95-143.

U.S. Department of Education. Office of Libraries and Learning Technologies. *Index to LSCA Documents.* August, 1980. (In-house Working Document.)

U.S. Department of Education. Office of Libraries and Learning Technologies. *Library Programs.* Washington, D.C.: Office of Libraries and Learning Technologies, 1980.

U.S. Office of Education. Office of Libraries and Learning Resources. State and Public Library Services Branch. *The State Plan of the Library Services and Construction Act; Concepts and Interrelationships of the State/Federal Agreement, the Long-Range Program, and the Annual Program.* (Guide for Administering LSCA, as Amended.) P. L. 84-597. April 1979.

U.S. Office of Education. Office of Libraries and Learning Resources. State and Public Library Services Branch. *Selecting and Using Criteria for Determining Adequacy of Public Library Services.* (Guide for Administering LSCA, as Amended.) P.L. 84-597. April 1979.

U. S. President. *Public Papers of the President. Richard M. Nixon.* "Special Message to the Congress on Education Priorities. January 24, 1974." Washington, D.C.: Government Printing Office, 1975, pp. 33-40. (Library Partnership Act, p. 39.)

U.S. Statutes at Large. Vol. 91. Public Law 95-123. "Library Services and Construction Amendments of 1977." 95th Congress. 1st Session. October 7, 1977.

Appendix A

THE LIBRARY SERVICES AND CONSTRUCTION ACT:

Legislative Chronology

6-19-56 - P.L. 84-597. Library Services Act (public library services for rural areas only).

8-1-56 - P.L. 84-896. Organic Act, added Guam to the list of Territories.

8-31-60 - P.L. 86-679. LSA extended for 5 years.

9-25-62 - P.L. 87-688. Added American Samoa.

2-11-64 - P.L. 88-269. Library Services and Construction Act. Added urban areas and Title II, Construction, and extended program to District of Columbia.

7-19-66 - P.L. 89-511. Extended 5 years, added Title III, Interlibrary Cooperation and Title IVA (Institutions) and IVB (Physically Handicapped). Added also the Trust Territory of the Pacific Islands.

11-24-67 - P.L. 90-154. Technical amendments, permitted acquisition of existing buildings for public library use as eligible expenditure under Title II.

12-30-70 - P.L. 91-600. Library Services and Construction Act. Amendments of 1970 extend for 5 years, consolidate Titles I, IVA, and IVB, emphasizes services to low-income families, provides for strengthening state library administrative agencies and metropolitan libraries which serve as national or regional resource centers; removes matching requirements for interlibrary cooperation, Title III; and streamlines state plan procedures.

147

5-3-73 -   P.L. 93-29. Library Services and Construction Act. Amended by the "Older Americans Comprehensive Services Amendments of 1973" to add a new Title IV, entitled "Older Readers Services." (This title has not been funded.)

10-19-73 - P.L. 93-133. Library Services and Construction Act. Amended by the "National Foundation on the Arts and the Humanities Amendments of 1973" to enlarge the definition of "public library" to include research libraries meeting specific criteria.

8-21-74 - P.L. 93-380. Library Services and Construction Act. Amended by the "Education Amendments of 1974" to add program priority for service to areas of high concentrations of persons of limited English-speaking ability.

10-7-77 - P.L. 95-123. Library Services and Construction Act. Amended to extend the program through 1982, and requires that: (1) federal funds spent for administration must now be matched with state or other non-federal funds; (2) the base year for meeting maintenance of effort requirements for services for handicapped and institutionalized persons be changed from FY 1971 to the second preceding fiscal year; and (3) additional emphasis be placed on strengthening major urban resource libraries.

Source: U.S. Office of Education, Office of Libraries and Learning Technologies, LSCA, 3/28/78

Appendix B

Federal Funds Under LSCA

Library Services Act; Library Services and
Construction Act, Title I, Federal Funds
FY 1957-1982

FY	Authorization	Administration request	Appropriation	Federal obligation
P.L. 84-597 - 6/19/56 LSA (public library services for rural areas only).				
P.L. 84-896 - 8/1/56 Added Guam.				
1957	$ 7,500,000	-0-	$ 2,050,000	$ 2,050,000
1958	7,500,000	3,000,000	5,000,000	4,436,674
1959	7,500,000	3,000,000	6,000,000	5,236,015
1960	7,500,000	6,650,000	7,500,000	6,098,559
P.L. 86-679 - 8/31/60 LSA. Extended for 5 years.				
1961	7,500,000	7,300,000	7,500,000	6,278,014
1962	7,500,000	7,500,000	7,500,000	7,062,670
P.L. 87-688 - 9/25/62 Added American Samoa.				
1963	7,500,000	7,500,000	7,500,000	7,406,406
P.L. 88-269 - 2/11/64 LSCA. Added urban areas and D.C., and Title II, Construction.				
1964	25,000,000	7,500,000	7,500,000	7,454,994
1965	25,000,000	25,000,000	25,000,000	25,000,000
1966	25,000,000	25,000,000	25,000,000	25,000,000
P.L. 89-511 - 7/19/66 LSCA. Added Title III, Interlibrary Cooperation and Title IVA (Institutions) and IVB (Physically Handicapped). Added Trust Territory of the Pacific Islands. Extended Act 5 years.				
1967	35,000,000	25,000,000	35,000,000	34,934,538
P.L. 90-154 - 11/24/67 Technical amendments; allow purchase of existing bldg. for public library.				
1968	45,000,000	35,000,000	35,000,000	34,971,725

Year					
1970	65,000,000	17,500,000	35,000,000	29,750,000	(2% reduction)[1]
1971	75,000,000	29,750,000	35,000,000	35,000,000	

P.L. 91-600 - 12/30/70 Consolidation: Titles IVA and IVB into Title I. Extended Act 5 years.

Year					
1972	112,000,000	15,719,000	46,569,000	46,569,000	(32,000,000 released 74)
1973	117,600,000	30,000,000	62,000,000	30,000,000	

P.L. 93-29 - 5/3/73 Added new Title IV, "Older Readers Services."
P.L. 93-133 - 10/19/73 Included "research" in definition of "public Library."

Year					
1974	123,500,000	-0-	49,155,500	44,155,500	(5% reduction)[1]
1975	129,675,000	25,000,000	49,155,000	49,155,000	

P.L. 93-380 - 8/21/74 Added priority for persons with limited English-speaking ability.

Year				
1976	137,150,000	10,000,000	49,155,000	49,155,000
1976TQ	0[2]	12,289,000	12,289,000	11,874,930
1977	0[2]	41,749,000	56,900,000	56,900,000 (est.)

P.L. 95-123 Extended Act 5 years. Added emphasis for urban libraries when appropriation exceeds $60 million for Title I. Amended "Maintenance of effort" for services to the institutionalized and the handicapped to second preceding year and required equal amount from non-federal funds when LSCA funds are used for administrative purposes.

Year				
1978	110,000,000	56,900,000	56,900,000	56,900,000
1979	140,000,000	56,900,000	62,500,000	62,500,000
1980	150,000,000	56,900,000	62,500,000	62,500,000
1981	150,000,000	62,500,000	62,500,000	62,500,000
1982	150,000,000	41,250,000	60,000,000	

[1] Percent reduction in OE Budget; LSCA Budget reduction was at higher level.
[2] Authorization in amendment, P.L. 91-600, expired on June 30, 1976.
Educational amendments of 1974 extended the legislation for one additional year expiring September 30, 1977.

Library Services and Construction Act, Title II, Federal Funds, FY 1964-1982

FY	Authorization	Administration request	Appropriation	Federal Obligation	Total Federal Obligation
1964	$20,000,000	-0-	-0-	-0-	-0-
1965	30,000,000	$30,000,000	$30,000,000	$29,863,755	$29,863,755
1966	30,000,000	30,000,000	30,000,000	29,778,368	29,778,368
1967	40,000,000	30,000,000	40,000,000	24,582,507	24,582,507
1968***	50,000,000	27,185,000[1]	27,185,000[1] [33,602,493]	15,157,893** 12,271,257	27,429,150
1969	60,000,000	9,185,000	9,185,000[2]	14,798,121** 7,458,966	22,257,087
1970	70,000,000	-0-	[24,098,743[2]] 7,807,250*[3] [9,561,643]	1,654,106** 3,379,643	5,033,943
1971	80,000,000	-0-	7,092,500[4] [11,519,913]	4,337,133** 4,233,471	8,570,604
1972	80,000,000	-0-	9,500,000[5] [12,359,629]	2,772,029** 6,761,037	9,533,066
1973	84,000,000	-0-	15,000,000[6] [2,738,963]	2,585,000**	2,585,000
1974	88,000,000	-0-	-0- [15,000,000]	10,636,985**	10,636,985
1975	92,500,000	-0-	-0- [4,363,015]	4,047,901**	4,047,901
1976	97,000,000	-0-	-0-	-0-	-0-
1977	-0-	-0-	-0-	-0-	-0-

1978	as may be necessary	-0-	-0-	-0-	-0-
1979	as may be necessary	-0-	-0-	-0-	-0-
1980	as may be necessary	-0-	-0-	-0-	-0-
1981	as may be necessary	-0-	-0-	-0-	-0-
1982	97,000,000	-0-	-0-	-0-	-0-

[1] Available for obligation fiscal year 1968; $15,417,493 carryover from fiscal year 1967 appropriation; plus $18,185,000 available for fiscal year 1968 appropriation. ($9,000,000 of the $27,185,000 was not made available until fiscal year 1969).

[2] Available for obligation fiscal year 1969; $14,913,743 carryover from fiscal year 1968 appropriation; plus $9,185,000 available from fiscal year 1969 appropriation. ($24,098,743).

[3] Available for obligation fiscal year 1970; $1,754,393 carryover from fiscal year 1969 appropriation plus $7,807,250 available from fiscal year 1970 appropriation of $9,185,000 after 2% reduction. ($9,561,643).

[4] Available for obligation fiscal year 1971; $4,427,000 carryover from fiscal year 1970 appropriation plus $7,092,500 fiscal year 1971 appropriation. ($11,519,913).

[5] Available for obligation fiscal year 1972; $2,859,629 carryover from fiscal year 1971 plus $9,500,000 available for fiscal year 1972 appropriation. ($12,359,629).

[6] Available for obligation fiscal year 1973; $2,738,963 carryover from fiscal year 1972. The $15,000,000 appropriated was not released until fiscal year 1974.

*After 2% reduction.

**Carryover funds from prior year.

***Beginning with 1968, amount in [brackets] was actual amount available for obligation in that year.

153

Library Services and Construction Act,
Title III, Federal Funds, FY 1967-1982

FY	Authorization	Administration request	Appropriation	Federal obligation
1967	$ 5,000,000	$ 375,000	$ 375,000	$ 352,000**
1968	7,500,000	2,375,000	2,375,000	2,060,908**
			(2,256,000)*	
1969	10,000,000	2,281,000	2,281,000	2,149,771
1970	12,500,000	2,281,000	2,281,000	2,079,126
1971	15,000,000	2,281,000	2,281,000	2,281,000
1972	15,000,000	2,730,000	2,640,500	2,625,000**
1973	15,750,000	-0-	7,500,000	7,500,000**
1974	16,500,000	-0-	2,593,500	2,593,500**
1975	17,300,000	-0-	2,594,000	2,594,000**
1976	18,200,000	-0-	2,594,000	2,594,000**
1976TQ	-0-¹	648,000	648,000	633,548**
1977	-0-¹	10,000,000	3,337,000	3,280,269**
1978	15,000,000	3,337,000	3,337,000	3,279,737**
1979	20,000,000	3,337,000	5,000,000	4,985,000**
1980	20,000,000	3,337,000	5,000,000	5,000,000**
1981	20,000,000	12,000,000	12,000,000	11,903,330**
1982	20,000,000	10,560,000	11,520,000	

¹ Authorization in amendment, P.L. 91-600, expired on June 30, 1976. Educational Amendments of 1974 extended the legislation for one additional year, expiring September 30, 1977.

*Available after 5% cutback.

**100% Federal funding - no matching required.

Library Services and Construction Act,
Title IVA, Federal Funds, FY 1967-1971***

FY	Authorization	Administration request	Appropriation	Federal obligation
1967	$ 5,000,000	$ 375,000	$ 375,000	$ 344,925**
1968	7,500,000	2,120,000	2,120,000	1,890,500***
			(2,014,000)*	
1969	10,000,000	2,094,000	2,094,000	1,953,596
1970	12,500,000	2,094,000	2,094,000	1,960,454
1971	15,000,000	2,094,000	2,094,000	2,094,000

*Available after 5% cutback.
**100% Federal funding through fiscal year 1968.
***Merged with Title I, FY 1972.

Library Services and Construction Act,
Title IVB, Federal Funds, FY 1967-1971***

FY	Authorization	Administration request	Appropriation	Federal obligation
1967	$3,000,000	$ 250,000	$ 250,000	$ 233,905**
1968	4,000,000	1,320,000	1,320,000	1,149,485***
			(1,254,000)*	
1969	5,000,000	1,334,000	1,334,000	1,227,229
1970	6,000,000	1,334,000	1,334,000	1,257,157
1971	7,000,000	1,334,000	1,334,000	1,334,000

*Available after 5% cutback
**100% Federal funding through fiscal year 1968.
***Merged with Title I, FY 1972.

Source: U.S. Office of Education. Office of Libraries and Learning Technologies. State and Public Library Services Branch, July 1979. Updated.

Index

157

Indices prepared by Ruth Gambee